Yes, Prime Minister

A comedy

Antony Jay and Jonathan Lynn

Samuel French — London
www.samuelfrench-london.co.uk

YES, PRIME MINISTER

A version of this play was first presented on 13 May 2010 at Chichester Festival Theatre with the following cast:

Sir Humphrey Appleby	Henry Goodman
Bernard Woolley	Jonathan Slinger
Jim Hacker	David Haig
Claire Sutton	Emily Joyce
Kumranistan Ambassador	Sam Dastor
Jeremy Burnham	William Chubb
Simon Chester	Tim Wallers

Directed by Jonathan Lynn
Designed by Simon Higlett
Lighting designed by Tim Mitchell
Casting Director: Gabrielle Dawes

Subsequently transferred to the Gielgud Theatre, London on 17 September 2010 with the same cast.

This later version of the play was presented at the Trafalgar Studios, London, on 6 June 2012 with the following cast:

Sir Humphrey Appleby	Michael Simkins
Bernard Woolley	Clive Hayward
Jim Hacker	Robert Daws
Claire Sutton	Emily Bruni
Kumranistan Ambassador	Sam Dastor
Jeremy Burnham	Tony Boncza
Simon Chester	Jim Barclay

Directed by Jonathan Lynn
Designed by Simon Higlett
Lighting designed by Tim Mitchell
Casting Director: Jonathan Russell

CHARACTERS

Sir Humphrey Appleby, Cabinet Secretary
Bernard Woolley, Principal Private Secretary
      to the Prime Minister
Jim Hacker, Prime Minister
Claire Sutton, Special Policy Adviser
Kumranistan Ambassador
Jeremy Burnham, Director-General of the BBC
Simon Chester, BBC presenter

SYNOPSIS OF SCENES

The action of the play takes place in the Prime Minister's study at Chequers, an English Tudor country mansion.

ACT I
SCENE 1 Autumn, late afternoon on a Friday
SCENE 2 The same day, after dinner

ACT II
SCENE 1 The action is continuous
SCENE 2 The following Sunday, morning

Set photographs from the Chichester Festival Theatre production of *Yes, Prime Minister* © Manuel Harlan

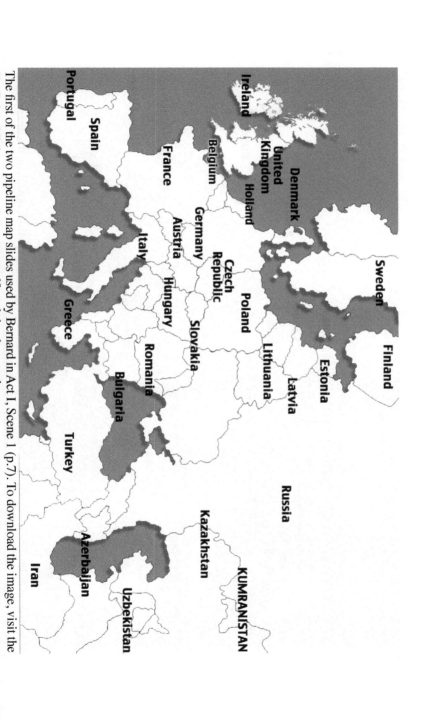

The first of the two pipeline map slides used by Bernard in Act I, Scene 1 (p.7). To download the image, visit the

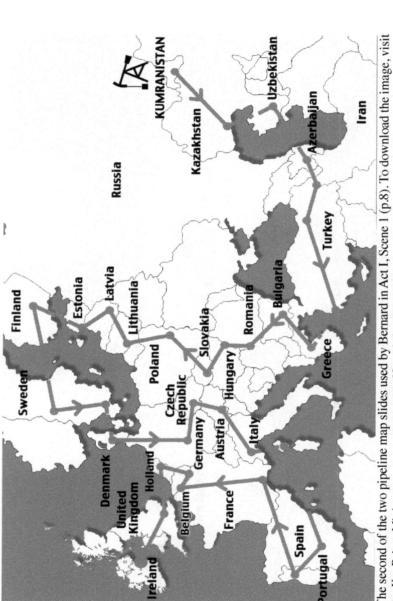

The second of the two pipeline map slides used by Bernard in Act I, Scene 1 (p.8). To download the image, visit the *Yes Prime Minister* page on www.samuelfrench-london.co.uk

ACT I

Scene 1

The Prime Minister's study at Chequers. Autumn, late afternoon on a Friday

The study is a comfortably furnished, panelled room at Chequers, an Elizabethan country mansion. It has a desk with a telephone and red binder on it, a chair, a seating area with a TV which is on and a remote, a coffee table, a side table, a globe, main double doors (stage centre, to the right), a smaller door (upstage left) and large windows looking out into the garden. Five red boxes containing files are stacked on top of each other on a chair or table

Sir Humphrey Appleby and Bernard Woolley are waiting. Humphrey is standing, Bernard is sitting, reading the "Evening Standard"

TV Newsreader And the main headline again: there is still no sign of agreement at the Lancaster House conference. The Prime Minister has denied that the European Union is sailing on the Titanic. And now, weather. Severe thunderstorms are forecast for London and the Home Counties ...

Using the remote, Humphrey switches off the TV. Bernard puts down the "Evening Standard"

Bernard It's awful, isn't it?
Humphrey What's awful, Bernard?
Bernard Well, all these jobs going. Repossessions. Fear of inflation.
Humphrey Oh yes. Terrible.
Bernard You don't sound terribly worried, Sir Humphrey.
Humphrey Bernard, I am not being sacked, repossessed or inflated. Neither are you.
Bernard Nor's the Prime Minister. But he's worried stiff.
Humphrey So he should be.
Bernard You don't sympathize with him?
Humphrey That's the deal. That's how Prime Ministers' careers go. They get to be on the front page every day for years, which they love.

They travel the long path from euphoric triumph to ignominious failure and then make way for the next saviour of the nation. It's called democracy.

Bernard It beats me why anyone would want to be Prime Minister.

Humphrey It's the only top job in the country that requires no previous experience. No training, no qualifications and limited intelligence.

Bernard Sir Humphrey ... You do believe in democracy, don't you?

Humphrey Do I, Bernard? Actually — no, not as most people understand it. Democracy should not be about executing the will of the people. It should be the process whereby we secure the consent of the people to the policies of those qualified to decide on their behalf.

Bernard Like who?

Humphrey Like us, Bernard!

Bernard I believe in democracy, Sir Humphrey.

Humphrey It does you credit. And if all the voters were as informed and intelligent as — say — me, or even you, it could possibly work. But that's hardly realistic.

Bernard Well, obviously we have to stop the government making stupid mistakes. If I did everything the Prime Minister told me to do, I'd be fired within a week, and rightly so. But I *am* there to help him.

Humphrey Bernard, we have a leadership crisis in this country. If the government can't or won't exercise it, it falls to us, whether we want it or not.

Bernard I know. Power abhors a vacuum.

Humphrey And we are currently led by one. It's even worse because he has no overall majority.

Bernard A hung parliament is a bad thing?

Humphrey Yes Bernard, hanging's too good for them.

Bernard At least the Coalition agreement that they came up with seems reasonable.

Humphrey Of course it is, Bernard, I wrote it for them. I managed to draft the coalition agreement so that we, in effect, are the elected government: if the government wants to do something silly we can make sure that their coalition partners stop them. And we *should* exercise power because we have nothing to gain or lose personally: we have respectable salaries, honours, an office and a chauffeur —

Bernard I haven't got a chauffeur ...

Humphrey You will, Bernard, when you grow up. We end up with an index-linked pension, a bank directorship, a couple of nicely remunerated quangos and a cottage in the Dordogne. So we can be entirely even-handed in our judgements and make them in the public interest.

Bernard Well, things may not seem so bad soon, when we tell the

Prime Minister about Kumranistan. (*He taps the binder on the coffee table*) European Central Bank to the rescue.
Humphrey Bernard! Do not mention the ECB to the Prime Minister.

During the next four speeches, Humphrey takes the file from Bernard and places it in a red box. Bernard puts other files on top, closes the box, and methodically piles the other four boxes on top of it

Bernard No, Sir Humphrey.
Humphrey And, whatever happens, don't let him know that the plan is dependent on joining the euro.
Bernard Well, it says so in the ECB proposal but not until page sixty-seven. He never gets beyond page three of anything. Then he jumps to the last paragraph.
Humphrey I hope you concealed the report properly.
Bernard Bottom of the fifth box. Inside a Vehicle Licensing Centre folder, like you told me. He'll never find it.
Humphrey It had better work. You know his views on Europe.
Bernard Yes, he's afraid that Brussels will take away most of his powers.
Humphrey They already have. And so they should.
Bernard Can't he stand up to them? Or would that be too controversial?
Humphrey It would be worse than controversial. It would be courageous.
Bernard That's worse?
Humphrey Oh yes. Being controversial loses you votes, being courageous can lose you the election. All we need him to do is preside at tonight's dinner, pretend he's read the Kumranistan plan, and leave the rest to us.

Jim Hacker enters right with a briefcase, in a hurry

He goes straight to his desk. So does Bernard, to help him unload his briefcase

Jim Sorry I'm late, it's been a terrible day.
Humphrey Any particular reason?
Jim You've read about the Cabinet split?
Humphrey Yes.
Jim You've seen what's happened to the Footsie?
Humphrey Yes.
Jim And the pound?
Humphrey Yes.
Jim And the inflation forecast?

4 Yes, Prime Minister

Humphrey Yes.

Jim The dreadful unemployment figures?

Humphrey Yes.

Jim *So how many particular reasons do you want?*

Humphrey Well ——

Jim And now this Lancaster House conference is turning into a catastrophe.

Humphrey But it was your idea to convene it, Prime Minister.

Jim Humphrey, if you become President of Europe in the middle of the biggest financial crisis for eighty years ——

Bernard Um — with respect, Prime Minister, there is no such title as President of Europe.

Jim You're so pedantic, Bernard, what's my official title then, President of the European Council?

Humphrey No Prime Minister, the Presidency of the European Council has gone to the Belgian Prime Minister.

Jim Who is completely unknown!

Humphrey *(with contempt)* Well, obviously! He's Belgian!

Jim And not elected. Appointed, in secret! 'Course, you wouldn't have a problem with that, would you Humphrey?

Humphrey You do me an injustice. I am all in favour of elections provided the right people do the voting.

Jim I can't understand it, I'm sure that I'm President of the Council. I was in the Chair.

Bernard Well it is a bit confusing, Prime Minister. You see we, the British, have the Presidency of the Council of the European Union which is held for six months by each country, not by individual leaders and not by you personally. The European Council and the Council of the European Union are not the same thing.

Jim So which of them really runs Europe?

Bernard Oh, neither!

Jim So who does?

Humphrey The President of the European Commission. But what it all boils down to for you, Prime Minister, is the difference between being head of an empire of five hundred million people and chairing the Council of Ministers for six months.

Jim Humphrey, we were talking about why I convened the conference on this dreadful recession. I had to do something.

Humphrey And the conference was something. So you did it! Well done.

Jim Exactly. But now it's falling apart, which might just about finish me.

Humphrey It may not be falling apart, Prime Minister.

Jim Haven't you been reading the conference reports?

Humphrey *I* have. Have you?

Jim The spadework wasn't done properly. The Foreign Office and the Treasury let me down badly. The Foreign Secretary and the Chancellor are probably plotting to get rid of me already.

Humphrey That's why I didn't suggest inviting them this weekend.

Jim Everyone knows that you have to agree the final bulletin before the conference begins. But instead of having everything nailed down before they all convened they left it to chance. Useless!

Bernard *"Forsan miseros meliora sequentur."*

Jim What?

Bernard "For those in misery, perhaps better things will follow."

Humphrey (*with a superior chuckle*) Ah yes, well said, Bernard.

Bernard *I* didn't actually say that. That was Virgil.

Humphrey I know that, Bernard.

Bernard At least I did say it, just now, but not originally.

Humphrey Thank you, Bernard, we get the point.

Jim It was completely predictable: the Krauts don't want a stimulus plan, they're terrified of runaway inflation because that's what destroyed the Weimar Republic and brought them Hitler. The Wops and the Dagoes are up to their armpits in debt already. The Frogs only want it if France gets the benefits ——

Bernard (*interrupting*) Prime Minister, I really think you should stop using these pejorative epithets to describe our allies, they might slip out in public sometime.

Jim Quire right, Bernard. Thank you. And the Micks and the Polacks aren't getting the subsidies they were promised, which they regard as a betrayal. So it's time for me to take a hands-on approach and give some leadership.

Humphrey Good.

Jim So — tell me what I should do.

Humphrey That's just the kind of leadership we need.

Jim Thank you, Humphrey.

Humphrey And we have good news for you, Prime Minister ...

Bernard Late last night we had a breakthrough at Lancaster House. A new player has appeared on the scene.

Jim (*excited*) The Americans? Are they coming after all?

Humphrey No, their position is immutable. They won't come to the conference because you wouldn't let them chair it.

Jim I can't let them chair a European conference, Humphrey, look at the map! (*He pours himself a Scotch*)

Humphrey It could become an intercontinental conference, if that would save the whole European financial system from melting down again.

Jim Don't be silly, Humphrey, I'd lose face.

Humphrey Oh yes, of course. Silly of me.

Bernard Prime Minister, Kumranistan has joined us.

Jim Has it? Good. (*A beat*) Have I heard of them?

Humphrey They have oil. Massive new reserves have been found there. They're offering a possible ten trillion dollar loan to Europe, secured against future purchases.

Jim But — that could solve everything.

Humphrey Yes.

Jim Save the conference!

Bernard Yes.

Jim Save Europe, in fact!

Humphrey } (*together*) Yes.
Bernard

Jim (*seeing the headlines*) "Triumph for the Prime Minister!" "Victory for the President of Europe!"

Humphrey Prime Minister, you're *not* the —

Jim (*firmly*) Victory for the *President of Europe*, Humphrey.

Bernard The Kumranistan deal may solve your problems.

Jim Great. Where do I sign?

Humphrey Well. We're not quite there yet. They do want something in exchange.

Bernard You know where Kumranistan is?

Jim Yes. (*A beat*) Well, sort of. You know, over there.

They stare at him

East. Of Suez.

Bernard It lies in Turkestan, north of Uzbekistan, Kazakstan and Afghanistan. (*He goes to the globe*) Here, in fact.

Jim As I said, exactly.

Humphrey They had been planning to take their oil to Europe through the Soviet pipeline.

Jim They're not Soviets any more, Humphrey. They're Russians. They haven't been Soviets for twenty years.

Humphrey They still are in spirit, and always will be.

Bernard But the um Russians want a pretty huge payment ...

Humphrey Which Kumranistan doesn't want to pay, especially since the Soviets will have their hands on the tap.

Bernard So, with a little prompting from us, Kumranistan came up with plan B: a pipeline through Turkey, Greece and southern Europe, avoiding Russia altogether.

Humphrey What they need is European agreement. And that's what they're prepared to lend us ten trillion dollars for.

Jim Why?

Humphrey They want a guarantee of future oil purchases by everyone in the EU.

Jim (*after a beat*) I don't get it.

Humphrey It's *awfully* simple, Prime Minister. Kumranistan will lend Europe the money to buy Kumranistan's oil.

Jim And Europe borrows another ten trillion? More debt!

Humphrey It's not a problem, it doesn't have to be repaid for years. We get the money now, interest free, and we repay it in the future when we buy the oil that we'll need anyway.

Jim So how do they make their money?

Humphrey Ah — well. We'll pay a premium on the oil ——

Jim Aha! I knew there was a catch ——

Humphrey But not for many years to come. When there'll be a different government.

Jim Oh, all right then. Are all the Europeans on board?

Humphrey They are. And the problems are what we've been negotiating, as you will have seen in your red boxes.

Jim stares blankly at the five red boxes

Jim Yes. Um — remind me.

Humphrey Well, as you'll doubtless remember, the Turks refused to cooperate unless they were admitted to the European Union. I see their point. I've always had a soft spot for Johnny Turk.

Jim Johnny Turk? (*He sniggers*) You're on first name terms then?

Humphrey (*chuckling mirthlessly*) Very droll, Prime Minister. Turkey is an important ally, the only Muslim country with a secular democracy. We *need* ——

Jim (*interrupting*) Johnny Turk, yes.

Bernard Germany, France and Italy were against the plan on principle.

Jim What changed their minds?

Humphrey A ten trillion dollar loan.

Bernard Actually, that surprised me, Sir Humphrey. Surely, if a principle was involved ...?

Humphrey I think you'll find ten trillion dollars is a bit above the going rate for principles in the EU, Bernard.

Jim What *was* the principle?

Humphrey They don't like Muslims.

Jim Ah.

Bernard Anyway, everything is agreed. Everyone gets a share in the construction.

Using a remote, Bernard lowers an electrically operated screen. Then he brings up the first of two slides, a map of Europe and the Near East

Here's the route.

He brings up a second slide of the first map but with a superimposed absurd zig-zag pipeline route through Kazakhstan, Azerbaijan, Turkey, Greece, Bulgaria, Romania, Hungary, Slovakia, Poland, Lithuania, Latvia, Estonia, Finland, Sweden, Denmark, Germany, Czech Republic, Austria, Italy, Corsica, Spain, Portugal, France, Belgium, Holland, United Kingdom and Republic of Ireland

Jim That looks pretty straightforward. We're saved! But why didn't I know about all this?

Humphrey It's top secret.

Jim Good God, Humphrey, I'm the Prime Minister!

Humphrey (*soothingly*) I know, Prime Minister, and what an excellent Prime Minister you are! But it had to be kept under wraps. If it had leaked this week, money markets would have gone mad ...

Jim I see. Well ... is that everything I need to know?

Bernard There is one other thing.

Humphrey (*warning*) Bernard ...

Jim gives Humphrey an inquiring look

Bernard A power group in Kumranistan still wants the Russian route.

Humphrey Ah. (*He relaxes*) Yes, Bernard's right, they don't want to upset the Soviets. It's understandable, they share a border. But the Kumranistani Foreign Secretary has come over here to offer the deal to us if we want it.

Jim Invite him to dinner! Tonight!

Bernard I did, Prime Minister.

Humphrey (*patiently spelling it out*) *That's* why we're *here*.

Jim And he can do the deal? Now?

Humphrey He has the authority. But he needs careful handling, they're very sensitive about respect.

Jim You get an awful lot of respect for ten trillion dollars. He can have all mine, for a start.

Humphrey Excellent, Prime Minister.

Humphrey exits

Bernard is following

Jim Bernard.
Bernard (*turning*) Yes, Prime Minister?
Jim There's something you're not happy about. What is it?
Bernard Oh. Um ... um ... I'm not sure I can ...
Jim Spit it out, Bernard.
Bernard Um — "*Timeo Danaos et dona ferentes.*"
Jim What?
Bernard "I fear the Greeks, especially when they bring gifts." Remember the Trojan Horse, Prime Minister.

Bernard exits

Jim (*puzzled*) The Greeks can't afford gifts. (*He gets out his Blackberry and dials*) Claire? You at Chequers yet? ... Come to my study please ... Now.

Jim rings off, hurries to the pile of red boxes and pulls the bottom box out from beneath the top four. He opens it and starts looking through all the files

Claire knocks on the door

Come in.

Claire enters. She is an intelligent, attractive university lecturer, now serving as Head of the Policy Unit at Ten Downing Street

Jim Ah. Claire.
Claire What's the agenda for the weekend?
Jim I'm not sure. Dealing with the Europeans is like herding cats. Being President of Europe isn't enough. Europe is an empire and it needs an emperor.
Claire (*amused*) Meaning you?
Jim (*with modesty*) Well, of course, it's not for me to ——
Claire *Please* don't ever say that to the BBC. Or anyone else, for that matter.
Jim What I want to know is, is this pipeline plan for real?
Claire Seems to be. But then, why wasn't the Foreign Secretary invited to Chequers?
Jim The Foreign Secretary?
Claire He does have an interest.

Jim His only interest is in pushing me overboard and taking my job.

Claire OK. But the Chancellor wasn't invited either ...

Jim Yes, Sir Humphrey advised me not to ask either of them.

Claire Why not?

Jim Because... there's something I don't know about this pipeline plan. What is it that Humphrey's not telling me?

Claire Let's look. Was that the bottom box?

Jim Of course.

Claire Try the file at the bottom.

Jim (*reading the label*) Vehicle Licensing Centre, Swansea. (*He opens it*) Yes! "Kumranistan Loan". (*He hands it to Claire. He wants her to find the answer*) Bernard was blathering about Trojan Horses.

Claire So he must be talking about the pipeline mechanics.

Jim I don't care about the mechanics, I'm not an engineer.

Claire Fiscal mechanics, Jim. Financial engineering. We can't run Europe without joining the euro ...

Jim Why not? We ran India without joining the rupee.

Claire (*with a sudden insight*) Perhaps Humphrey has arranged for the proposed loan to go through the European Central Bank, and isn't mentioning it.

Jim Would that matter?

Claire Yes. If so, if we want any of the loan we'd have to join the euro.

Jim What?!? We can't join the euro! It would be a catastrophe! Hand over control of interest rates? Control of exchange rates? Control of money supply? When I need to inflate to get re-elected, if the Germans are worried about rising prices the ECB might deflate and I could get kicked out!

Claire Candidly, I'm not sure if that would bother Sir Humphrey.

Jim Well, let's find out. (*He picks up phone*) Yes, tell Sir Humphrey that I want to see him ... No, any time within the next *ten seconds* will do. (*He slams the phone down*)

Claire I think I'll disappear.

Claire slips out of the upstage door

Humphrey knocks and enters

Jim Ah, Humphrey, do sit down.

Humphrey Prime Minister.

Jim Let's talk about this loan. It is all good news, isn't it?

Humphrey Tremendous news.

Jim There are no hidden snags? You know. Terms and conditions,

penalty clauses, tough guarantees?
Humphrey Oh no. Nothing like that. Standard agreement.
Jim Great. An ordinary treasury loan. As far as we're concerned?
Humphrey In a sense. Yes.
Jim (*pouncing*) In a sense?
Humphrey In due course. Following agreed procedures. After certain formalities.
Jim But the money goes straight to the Treasury?
Humphrey It goes to the Treasury, yes.
Jim *Straight* to the Treasury?
Humphrey Broadly speaking, yes. More or less.
Jim Broadly speaking? How would you describe it if you were narrowly speaking?

Humphrey is silent

Does it have to go through the European Central Bank?
Humphrey We get the money, that's what matters.
Jim Let me put this another way. Will the loan be in euros?
Humphrey Prime Minister, I urge you not to clutter your mind with procedural detail and monetary trivia.
Jim Humphrey. In words of one syllable, is this plan dependent on our abandoning sterling and joining the euro?
Humphrey (*chuckling*) De-pen-dent has three syllables and a-ban-don-ing has four. Seriously, though, Prime Minister ... (*checking his watch*) ... it's almost time for your dinner with the Foreign Minister of Kumranistan, you really mustn't be late.
Jim Humphrey! Answer my question.
Humphrey All right, Prime Minister, you've asked a straight question and I'll give you a straight answer which, however, clearly has to be considered in its proper context. In the course of all financial negotiations, certain provisos have to be pre-cogitated and preconditioned, various caveats have to be postulated, designated, investigated and specified and a number of unequivocal considerations have to be determined, acknowledged and indeed sometimes conceded so that we are able to facilitate the finalization of preliminary plans to create an epistemological basis for all parties to proceed towards a mutually beneficial consummation which will acknowledge and safeguard the vital interests of all the participants without jeopardizing in any material way the underlying collective benefit ultimately accruing to the signatories or leaving unresolved certain anomalies and irregularities that might precipitate operational uncertainties down the line, so that there will be a presumed modicum of ironclad reciprocity which,

in the broad scheme of things, will be to everybody's advantage.

Jim Did that mean yes or no?

Humphrey Don't you think yes and no are rather broad and unspecific in their application?

Jim No. I don't. I want a clear unambiguous answer.

Humphrey Certainly. (*A beat*) What was the question again?

Jim Is joining the euro a condition of getting the loan?

Humphrey Well, in the sense that, if an agreement is, at the end of the day and depending on how ——

Jim Humphrey!

Humphrey (*penitent*) Yes it is.

Jim And you were going to hide this from me until it was too late!

Humphrey No, but, yes, I mean, they all insisted ... the ECB insisted ... Prime Minister, it is the only way! You need this deal. I did it for *you*!

Jim For me?

Humphrey Prime Minister, I'm trying to save you from yourself.

Jim Humphrey, why *on earth* would you want to join the euro *now*?

Humphrey Same reasons: European unity, the loan ——

Jim Another austerity package. Disastrous interest rates, public expenditure cuts, more interference from Brussels in every damn thing ... No ECB. No euro. Or no deal!

Humphrey But the Germans will have so many objections.

Jim Ten trillion dollars worth of objections?

Humphrey is silent

As I thought. And you were just going to let them get away with it? It would be the ultimate victory for Brussels. Britain becomes an outpost of the collapsing European empire.

Humphrey Of which you're the President.

Jim Don't be silly Humphrey, I just chair meetings for six months.

Humphrey If you would just take another look at the computer models ——

Jim No. Computer models got us *into* this whole financial mess to start with.

Humphrey That's different. Nobody knew that those computer models in the City were being given faulty information. Everyone assumed the mortgages were worth their face value.

Jim But they were worth nothing! Why didn't anyone know? Why didn't *you* know?

Humphrey (*humiliated*) Everyone thought that everyone else understood what was going on and nobody wanted to admit that they couldn't make sense of it.

Jim Why couldn't they?

Humphrey Because it didn't make sense! Everybody thought that all the others knew, and there *were* some who knew, but the ones who didn't know didn't believe that the ones who *did* know *knew*.

Jim Say that again?

Humphrey Nobody wanted to rock the boat because everyone was making so much money!

Jim Computer models, Humphrey, are no different from fashion models: seductive, unreliable, easily corrupted and they lead sensible people to make fools of themselves. And because you believed the computer models about the euro you tried to bounce your plan past me, and not tell me until it was too late. I'm appalled. I really don't know if we can go on working together.

Humphrey Prime Minister!

Jim I always thought I could trust you.

Humphrey (*anguished*) You can!

Jim Quite frankly, I'm now profoundly suspicious of this whole pipeline plan. I mean, I don't know what else I don't know. Do you know?

Humphrey Do I know what you don't know?

Jim Yes. Is there anything else I don't know that I should know?

Humphrey I — I hardly know where to begin.

Jim About this plan, I mean!

Humphrey regains control of himself

Humphrey Prime Minister, you know everything that you need to know. If you want the loan, if you don't want your premiership to crash on take-off, this is the way it has to be

Bernard knocks and enters

Bernard Drinks with Mr Aitikeev, the Kumranistani Foreign Secretary, are in five minutes, Prime Minister.

Jim Thank you, Bernard. At least I can believe what you tell me.

Jim looks bitterly at Humphrey, and exits

Humphrey Shut the door.

Bernard goes to the door — and continues through the doorway

From the inside!

Bernard comes back in and shuts the door

Bernard, did you tell the Prime Minister about joining the euro?

Bernard Absolutely not, Sir Humphrey, you asked me not to.

Humphrey Well, what put him on to it?

Bernard Perhaps it was his Special Adviser.

Humphrey That woman? How did she get here without your knowing?

Bernard I expect he called her on his BlackBerry.

Humphrey Bernard! You're letting him make his own appointments? If you lose control over his diary, you lose control over him! You never know where it'll end. He'll start running the country.

Bernard He can't. He doesn't know how to.

Humphrey Of course he doesn't. So he must be stopped.

Bernard What can I do about it?

Humphrey Get rid of his *BlackBerry*, Bernard!

Bernard How?

Humphrey Give me yours.

Bernard hands over his BlackBerry

Now get me a paper-clip.

Bernard gets one from Jim's desk. Humphrey straightens it

Humphrey You slide off the back plate. Take out the battery. See that hole? It's the re-set button. Push it in there. Right. Now it's buggered for days.

Bernard takes back his BlackBerry and checks it. Humphrey is right

Bernard Sir Humphrey! I had no idea you understood technology.

Humphrey I understand survival. You can practise while I'm at the dinner.

Humphrey exits

Black-out

Jim and Claire are enjoying drinks after dinner

It is now dark outside

Jim Dinner went well, I thought. They liked my speech.
Claire And they really liked the goulash and dumplings.

Jim gives her a sharp look

They liked your speech too. I'm sure they did.
Jim What did you make of the Kumranistani Foreign Minister? You think he's really going to come up with this loan?
Claire With the Kumranistanis, it's all about personal relationships. Trust. Confidence. Respect. Plus, he really liked the goulash so that's a good start, so much better than the usual rubber chicken.
Jim After he's on board we'll just need a few endorsements.
Claire Endorsements?
Jim Yes, remember the World Economic Forum at Davos? That really worked because Bob Geldof came out in support of it.
Claire I know, we're working on that. And Annie Lennox, and Bono.
Jim (*he's a fan*) Bono. Oh, great!

Bernard enters

Jim Hello, Bernard. Enjoy dinner?
Bernard I wasn't there, I was busy with — other things.
Jim Pity, you'd have enjoyed my speech.
Bernard I'm sure, Prime Minister, but I heard the goulash was good.

Now Jim gives Bernard a sharp look. He feels undermined but decides not to mention anything

Jim New cook, apparently.
Bernard Yes and — um — in connection with that, we have a situation. Unfortunately we've just discovered the cook here is in the UK illegally.
Claire (*instantly alert*) We have an illegal immigrant working at Chequers?
Jim How? What the hell is the Home Office doing?
Bernard I wonder if anyone will ever solve that perennial riddle.
Jim Plotting against me, I should imagine. The Home Secretary wants my job.

Claire They all do.

Jim I think I'll reshuffle her to the graveyard: the Ministry of Culture, Media and Sports. There's no coming back from there.

Bernard I've never understood the connection between those three.

Jim Cuture, media and sports? None of them matter.

Bernard What do I do about this cook?

Jim Where's she from?

Bernard She wouldn't say, apparently, but she's got a false EU passport.

Jim Can't we just rush a visa through for her?

Bernard I'll try, but if you're right about the Home Office it'll take months. I think we have to let her go.

Jim Right. We can't risk the media finding out. "PRIME MINISTER HARBOURS ILLEGAL IMMIGRANT!" How did it come to light?

Bernard One of the waiters mentioned it at dinner.

Jim Somebody's probably phoned the BBC already.

They all laugh. The phone rings. Bernard answers it and listens

Bernard It's the BBC ...

Jim stands — his unfinished whisky is left on the coffee table

(*On the phone*) Oh, I see. Fine. (*He hangs up*) That was actually the Press Office. BBC Television's devoting their Sunday morning programme to you, Prime Minister.

Jim Devoting it to me?

Bernard No other stories. A full hour about you.

Jim Should I be pleased?

Bernard I fear not. It will be called "Government In Crisis".

Jim Christ!

Bernard They want to interview you about the rumoured Cabinet reshuffle and the deadlock in the Summit at Lancaster House.

Claire You're not going to do that, Jim. (*To Bernard*) He's not doing that.

Jim If I could mention the Kumranistan loan ——

Claire You can't! Not until Kumranistan has definitely signed on the dotted line and not until this euro business with the European Central bank is sorted out.

Jim Phone them back. Pretend to be helpful.

Claire Whatever they ask, just give them one of the replies in the red binder by the phone.

Bernard crosses to the phone and peruses the red binder with interest

Bernard I haven't seen this before.
Jim Supplied by the Press Office.
Claire At my suggestion. I worked on it with them.
Bernard Good. Right. (*He dials*) Yes ... may I speak to Robin Simpson? (*He listens*) Yes, it's Bernard Woolley here, the Prime Minister's Principal Private Secretary ... He can't speak to you himself, but how can I help?

He presses the speakerphone button so that Jim and Claire can hear
Robin (*v.o.*) Well, it seems he is losing the support of his cabinet and his backbenchers.
Claire Number three.

Bernard turns to page 3 and reads a reply from the red binder

Bernard "The Prime Minister is not interested in Westminster tittletattle. He has the full support of his colleagues and his party on all matters of substance. It's business as usual."
Robin (*v.o.*) I see. But has the Prime Minister thought of resigning in the interests of party unity?
Bernard (*turning the page*) You're *seriously* asking me that?
Claire Number four.

Jim joins Claire on the sofa and reads the red binder with her. Claire lip-mimes along with Bernard

Bernard "The Prime Minister was elected to do a job and he intends to get on with it. It will mean tough decisions but that's what the country expects and that's what he's going to do." (*He smiles happily at Claire*) Next?
Robin (*v.o.*) What about the awful state of the economy?
Jim
Claire } (*together*) Number one!

Jim now lip-mimes along too

Bernard "This isn't a British crisis, it's a *world* crisis. Many countries are worse affected than we are. We intend to play our part within the Community."
Robin (*v.o.*) But what exactly is he doing about it?
Jim Two?

Claire nods

(*to Bernard*) Two.

Bernard (*into the phone*) Number Two. (*Reading*) "The government will do everything that needs to be done. He will not flinch from his duty and a statement will be made when the time is ripe."

Robin (*v.o.*) Why do you think the European Financial summit has got nowhere?

Bernard I don't think that.

Jim
Claire } (*together*) FIVE!

Bernard What?

Jim
Claire } (*together*) FIVE!

Robin (*v.o.*) Is the Prime Minister there?

Bernard No, sorry, that's the TV you can hear. (*He mouths "Shhhh" as he switches off the speakerphone and turns a page*) Um ... "The Prime Minister was elected to do a job and —— " Oh no, not that, I've done that one already ... (*Flipping the page to read number 5*) "The meeting-stroke-conference has certainly not been a failure. There has been invaluable groundwork and a blueprint has been drawn up for the next phase. Rome wasn't built in a day!" (*He listens*) Thank you.

Jim What are you thanking her for?

Bernard (*with his hand over the mouthpiece*) She says I've been thoroughly unhelpful.

Jim Well done. Well done, both of you. (*He pours himself a Scotch*)

Bernard (*into the phone*) What? (*To Jim*) "How happy is the Prime Minister about his future?"

Jim He's as happy as a rat-catcher on a rubbish dump.

Bernard The Prime Minister is as happy as an environmental health officer on a civic amenity site. (*He hangs up*)

Jim I hate the BBC. Nasty, rude, arrogant, aggressive, ungrateful people who all think they could do better than me. It's like having three Oppositions: one at Westminster and two others at Broadcasting House and the TV Centre.

The phone rings. Bernard gets it

Bernard Yes? ... Oh, Ms Simpson again ... What kind of leak? ... About joining the euro?

Jim and Claire are all ears

Bernard No, the Prime Minister knows nothing about this. Britain's position on the euro is unchanged....No, I can't explain the markets, who can? (*He rings off*)

Jim Let's get online. (*He puts his whisky down on the coffee table, picks up his BlackBerry and presses some keys*) My BlackBerry doesn't seem to be working.

Bernard (*pretending surprise*) Good heavens! Mine isn't either!

Claire Mine is. Oh. This is interesting. The rumours started after heavy buying of euros by Golding Brothers Bank. Funny.

Jim Why?

Claire Humphrey's got a directorship lined up there when he retires.

They all look at each other

Jim He's out of control.

Bernard It might have been someone else.

Jim Who else knew? Even I didn't know.

They all think

Bernard Shall I get Sir Humphrey?

Claire Has he gone to bed?

Bernard When last seen, he was drowning his sorrows in a glass of The Glenlivet in the Long Gallery.

Jim (*still thinking*) As there's been heavy buying of the euro ... that would explain today's heavy selling of the pound.

Claire Yes.

Jim I must do something!

Claire and Bernard wait to see what he is going to suggest. But he says nothing more

Bernard (*after a glance at Claire*) You know, I'm sure Sir Humphrey wouldn't leak.

Jim He's tried to bounce us into Europe and feather his nest by briefing the bank. I've got to get him under control. He's an over-mighty subject.

Bernard Actually, he's the Queen's subject, not yours, you're just the ——

Jim I know who I am, Bernard! Claire, it's just one more example of the corruption of those who think they're above the law. We've started to curb the MPs, now we must deal with the Civil Service.

Claire Suits me. We've had that paper ready for a while.

Bernard (*instantly worried*) What paper?

Claire Reform of the Civil Service, root and branch.

Bernard Oh! That paper.
Jim So we have. Where is it, Bernard?
Bernard (*immediately*) It's gone.
Jim What do you mean, "gone"?

Claire goes to Jim's desk

Bernard Lost. Discredited. Shredded. One of those. Can't remember
exactly.
Jim Bernard ——
Bernard It really wasn't very good. Too general. Badly argued. Imprac-
ticable, over-specific ——
Jim Too general and over-specific?
Claire (*beside Jim again*) I kept a copy in your desk, Jim. (*She hands
it to him*)

Jim leafs through it

Jim Oh yes. (*He chuckles*) That will really cramp their style. Clip their
wings. (*He chuckles*) Tie their hands.
Bernard Nothing has hands and wings, Prime Minister.
Claire Except angels.
Bernard Oh. Good point.
Jim Sorry Bernard, but the party will love this. So will the MPs, it'll
deflect attention from all their little fiddles and diddles. Get Humphrey
in, Bernard.

Bernards, exits, glum

Jim The country will love it too. It's a winner.
Claire Jim, just remember the old rule: never corner the rat, it may bite.
Give him an escape route.

Bernard enters

Bernard He's coming.

Humphrey enters

Jim Ah, Humphrey, sit down.

He does

We've been talking about this leak.

Humphrey What leak, Prime Minister?

Jim About joining the euro. Surely you've heard? It's all round the City, apparently.

Humphrey Oh. That. Yes, well ——

Jim What can you tell me about it?

Humphrey I, Prime Minister? Nothing, except I'm told there are these rumours. Happens all the time.

Jim This is different. Hardly anybody knew your plan. Then Golding Brothers Bank started buying wads of euros this afternoon. Who tipped them off?

Humphrey If anyone did, we'll never find out.

Jim Oh, I think we will. Where did you have lunch yesterday, Humphrey?

Humphrey I can't remember.

Bernard It was Le Gavroche, Sir Humphrey.

Humphrey Oh yes, Le Gavroche. Thank you, Bernard. Why?

Jim On your own?

Humphrey I, er, I don't recall ... now who was it?

Jim You don't remember that either?

Humphrey One has so many lunches.

Jim (*helpfully*) One a day, in fact.

Humphrey Yes.

Jim I understand. Bernard, ring Le Gavroche and ask the Head Waiter who Sir Humphrey had lunch with yesterday.

Bernard heads for the phone

Humphrey Oh yes, I remember now. Some friends.

Jim Who were they?

Humphrey Just friends.

Jim Not directors of Golding Brothers Bank?

Humphrey Prime Minister, one does not cross-examine one's friends about what directorships they may happen to hold.

Jim Well, we can easily find out.

Humphrey What is the point, exactly?

Jim The point is, there is bound to be suspicion in cases like this.

Humphrey I can't see why. Surely you know, Prime Minister, that the Civil Service will always do what is best for the country.

Jim What about the government?

Humphrey I presume the government will too.

Jim Right. And you think this air of suspicion isn't fair on loyal public servants?

Humphrey It certainly isn't.

Jim I agree. So I've decided to introduce a new Civil Service Reform Act.

Humphrey What?!

Jim Yes, I think you'll be very happy about this. It will include a ban on any related jobs for civil servants for five years after they retire. No revolving door any more, no paid directorships, no paid consultancies ——

Humphrey But that's absurd! Men of great wisdom, great experience, leading figures of their generation, so much to offer ——

Jim And they can offer it, Humphrey. *Pro bono.* (*To Bernard*) Latin, Bernard.

Bernard *Pro bono publico*, actually.

Jim Exactly. All that wisdom and experience can be offered to the unpaid voluntary sector, Humphrey, for the public good. It will remove all temptation to betray government confidences to commercial employers. That'll be a relief, won't it?

Humphrey But there's never been a problem. We have a clearance committee. Everything has to be approved by it.

Jim Who appoints the members?

Humphrey Um ...

Bernard (*coming to the rescue*) There's an established procedure.

Claire You appoint them, Sir Humphrey.

Humphrey Do I? Oh yes, dear lady, so I do. As it happens.

Jim So that will be another burden off your shoulders. We'll appoint an independent clearance czar.

Humphrey Not another czar, please, Prime Minister. In the last three years we've appointed an enterprise czar, a youth crime czar, a welfare czar, a pre-school supremo, an unemployment watchdog, a banking regulator, A science and technology supremo and a community policing czar. If you go on like this you won't need a cabinet.

Jim Perfect!

Humphrey Perfect? Prime Minister, we even have a Twitter czar.

Bernard (*helpfully*) Her appointment was announced as a Tweet.

Humphrey What's she supposed to achieve? None of these people have achieved anything.

Jim They achieved their objective: at least twelve column inches in every paper. Merely by announcing them, their objective was achieved — it showed we were responsive, we were doing something, and it shut the press up.

Claire *And* it didn't cost anything.

Humphrey The Twitter Czar earns a hundred and sixty thousand pounds a year!

Jim Cheap at the price, headline news everywhere.

Bernard It would have cost much more if we'd actually set them up with offices and staff.

Claire And that would have meant more index-linked pensions.

Jim Right! Which is something else that the Civil Service Reform Act will address.

Bernard My God! You don't mean that?

Humphrey You'd get rid of index-linked pensions? You wouldn't want to do that to the nurses, would you? Or the dedicated teachers, the courageous policemen, the gallant firemen ...

Claire The starving permanent secretaries?

Humphrey (*laughing mirthlessly*) Very droll, dear lady. Prime Minister, I agree that there are aspects of the organization and administration of the public sector which could certainly benefit from measured consideration in the context of changing circumstances and the structural metamorphosis precipitated by the communications revolution, but it is important to bear in mind that administrative practical conditions of service have evolved over many years with manifold and complex interrelationships, and any attempt to vary one of them could have serious and unforeseeable effects on others, so to that end I would propose setting up a series of interdepartmental committees ——

Jim No, Humphrey! No time for interdepartmental committees. But there is one other change that I'd welcome your views on.

Humphrey Prime Minister?

Jim Would you call yourself a generalist? With your degree in classics?

Humphrey Indeed I would, Prime Minister. First class degree, actually.

Bernard Me too.

Jim Claire got a double first. And what was the title of your PhD thesis at Cambridge?

Claire "The Civil Service: The Pretence and the Practice."

Humphrey Most impressive, dear lady!

Jim It was published by the University Press.

Humphrey Such a pity that publishers are having such a struggle to survive nowadays, I wonder why.

Jim The point is, I was over at the Ministry of Defence yesterday. I find them rather impressive, don't you?

Humphrey (*warily*) I do, Prime Minister.

Jim What was really impressive was that they knew what they were talking about. They were qualified professionals. Soldiers, generals, admirals: experienced commanders. All our other government departments are staffed by historians and literature graduates — and classicists.

Humphrey Excellent. Men with the wisdom of the ages.

Jim No, Humphrey. Amateurs.

Humphrey (*aghast*) Amateurs?

Jim We should have teachers at the Department of Education, doctors and nurses at the Department of Health, accountants and actuaries at the Treasury. Experts. People who actually know what needs to be done.

Humphrey I think that would be very dangerous, Prime Minister.

Jim I want advice from real people, who live in the real world doing the real jobs ...

Humphrey Prime Minister, you're striking at the very heart of our whole system of government. Our success is founded upon staying free from the taint of professionalism. And the corruption of specialist knowledge. You're not seriously ... you can't be serious ... it's out of the question ... you wouldn't really do this? Would he, Bernard?

Bernard shrugs helplessly

Jim I would. But if we're not getting the Kumranistan loan we won't be needing to pass a special Finance Act which would free up parliamentary time to pass the Civil Service Act instead.

Humphrey glimpses light at the end of the tunnel

Humphrey Ah. You mean, if the European Central Bank agreed that the loan could go direct to the individual countries ...?

Jim In their chosen currency ... yes, the Civil Service Act would go on the back burner. But you said they wouldn't agree.

Humphrey I didn't think they'd agree ... But I could be wrong.

Jim (*smiling beatifically*) Say that again?

Humphrey (*tight-lipped*) I said "I could be wrong". (*He stands up*) Leave it with me, Prime Minister. (*Snapping*) Bernard!

Humphrey stalks out, with Bernard trailing unhappily behind him. Jim pours another Scotch

Claire Well played, Jim. Bernard's in trouble, though, for not heading this off.

Jim Do you think Humphrey can square the Central Bank?

Claire I think so. The Europeans don't give a toss how the money arrives as long as there's a lot of it and they get it quickly.

Jim So all that business about joining the euro ...?

Claire I think it was just a try-on.

Jim Why is he so keen on Europe *now*? It makes no sense.

Claire Because it moves power away from the vote-grubbing politicians and ignorant voters and over to appointed commissioners and unelected officials. Like him.

Jim Is that why he leaked this to his banking chums?

Claire No, I doubt if he meant to. I expect he was just sucking up to them, showing how useful he could be. He was probably horrified when they started buying euros.

Jim He's going to have some explaining to do when they realize we're not joining.

Claire He'll find a way.

Humphrey knocks on the door and enters

Humphrey I've had a quick word with the Head of the ECB, Prime Minister.

Jim (*amused*) Already? That was quick.

Humphrey Um, yes. He's talking to everyone.

Jim Good. So if they all agree, we may actually have this loan in place. Nothing else can go wrong tonight, can it?

Humphrey I don't see how, Prime Minister.

Bernard hurries in, looking worried

Bernard Prime Minister ——

Jim Cheer up, Bernard, have a drinkie, it looks as though your index-linked pension may be safe after all.

Bernard No, Prime Minister — I'm — um — I'm afraid we have a ... a situation.

Jim Can't it wait till the morning?

Bernard No, it can't. We have a problem. With the Kumranistani Foreign Secretary.

Claire Mr Aitikeev?

Jim Nice chap.

Bernard (*very doubtful*) Yes — well ... (*He shuts the door*) He just buttonholed me in the hall. It seems that Mr Aitikeev wants us to provide a ... um, sexual entertainment for him for tonight.

Jim What a prat!

Claire That's really not our problem, Bernard. Or yours.

Jim I always said he was a prat, didn't I?

Bernard Yes, Prime Minister.

Humphrey Boundaries have to be drawn, Bernard.

Bernard I know, Sir Humphrey — Prime Minister, with respect, it is our problem. I — I confess I didn't handle it as diplomatically as I should have. I'm afraid he felt slighted. He indicated that unless we find him what he wants he won't sign the contract tomorrow.

Claire What?!

Jim My God!

Jim stands, putting his whisky on the coffee table

Humphrey How did this happen?

Jim Why didn't you say you'd try to find him someone?

Bernard I should have, but frankly I was a little shocked.

Humphrey You always were a prig, Bernard.

Bernard If you say so, Sir Humphrey.

Claire So go back to Mr Aitikeev and tell him you're working on it.

Bernard How, exactly?

Humphrey (*to Claire*) Yes, how, exactly? This is Chequers, not Soho.

Claire Surely Bernard can get a girl up from London?

Bernard (*aghast*) Me?

Jim Are you serious? What about all the security at the gate?

Claire Don't use the gate. It's only twenty minutes from the West End to Chequers by helicopter. They check it before departure, but nobody checks it on arrival.

Jim And where do suggest we get a chopper at this time of night?

Bernard We do have an RAF helicopter standing by this weekend. The one the Queen uses.

Jim Do I understand this *correctly*? You want us to bring a call girl here, in the *royal helicopter*? For the Kumranistan Foreign Minister? Would you say that's an appropriate use of taxpayers' money?

Humphrey, Bernard and Claire consider

Claire Well, we do want the deal signed tomorrow, don't we?

Humphrey and Bernard nod

Got any better ideas?

Humphrey I think we should talk to Mr Aitikeev about this.

Jim Who should?

Humphrey You should.

Jim I'm not doing it.

Humphrey The Foreign Secretary's his opposite number, but you didn't invite him this weekend. Clearly you should have. Claire can't do it, she's a woman. You out-rank him, so it has to be you.

Jim I can't possibly do it. This conversation is for an underling like you, Humphrey.

Humphrey stiffens at the insult

I have to be able to deny all knowledge of it.

Humphrey Oh, perhaps you're right. Then I suggest that, as Mr Aitikeev spoke to Bernard, and as he's the Private Secretary, Bernard should talk to him. I think that would be the diplomatic protocol.

Bernard Um — I can't seem to recall any diplomatic protocol that specifies the Principal Private Secretary does the pimping.

Jim Well — OK, not you yourself, maybe, one of your people.

Bernard I don't have any people here. And Prime Minister, we absolutely can't let anyone else in on this.

Jim Why not?

Bernard I'm ... I'm — um — afraid there's more.

Jim More?

Bernard He has specific — tastes.

Jim You mean, like blonde or brunette?

Bernard Not exactly.

Jim What? You mean, a ginger?

Bernard No sir.

Claire Well what? Big boobs? Small boobs? Big bum? — WHAT?

Humphrey
Jim } (*together*) Is he gay?

Bernard If *only* it were that simple.

Jim Bernard, what sort of woman does he want?

Bernard Not a woman. (*He hesitates*) Three women.

Jim Three women?

Bernard Yes, Prime Minister. (*He hesitates*) More if possible. (*He hesitates again*) An orgy.

Jim is shocked

Jim I can't believe my ears.

Bernard Preferably one European, one Asian and one black.

Claire At least it's equal opportunities fornication.

Jim Claire, this isn't funny.

Claire Sorry.

Bernard He said that's what they did at the International Monetary Fund conferences with Dominique Strauss Kahn.

Humphrey We're not the IMF. We don't have a budget for this sort of thing.

Jim And we're accountable to the taxpayer. We can't have anything to do with this.

Bernard Of course not, Prime Minister! So, what do you suggest I do?
He says if we don't do this for him the whole deal's off.

Jim How *dare* you bring such a disgusting proposition to me!

Bernard I'm sorry, Prime Minister. Should I have just let the deal and
the summit conference collapse?

*Humphrey sits, shaking his head. Jim decides to evade Bernard's
question*

Jim How did he mention it? Was he embarrassed?

Bernard He said he was making a request in total confidence. I assured
him that I'm extremely discreet. Then he told me. I thought I must
have misheard so I asked him to repeat it. He did. I'm afraid he saw
the look on my face. He got angry. Made some threats. Told me to see
to it or else.

Jim You should have said it just wasn't possible.

Bernard I did. He said they got a man on the moon, we can get three
girls from King's Cross.

Claire I suppose that's technically true.

Jim But hardly the point, Claire.

Bernard Apparently he's also friends with Mr Berlusconi. He went to
several of his bunga-bunga parties.

Humphrey Claire, can Aitikeev really wipe out months of diplomacy?

Claire (*taking her whisky from the coffee table*) It wouldn't take much
— a word here, a word there, a hint of lost confidence — this whole
thing's very finely balanced.

Jim Aitikeev wants this deal, right?

Claire Yes, but he lost face with Bernard. Losing face is a big thing for
simple people.

Jim Claire, won't Aitikeev lose face if the deal falls apart?

Claire No. You will.

Jim Why not him?

Claire He's still got the Russian route if he wants.

Jim He certainly won't get any more weapons if he screws us over.

Humphrey Maybe Aitikeev doesn't care about the weapons. Maybe it's
just his President who wants them.

Claire Internal repression? That's a possibility.

Jim Doesn't Aitikeev have to account to his President if this all goes
south?

Claire Theoretically. But Aitikeev's here and the President's over
there.

Humphrey There's another possibility. Maybe Aitikeev's bluffing.

Maybe it's a test.
Jim A test? Of what?
Humphrey Of our friendship.
Jim We hardly know him.
Humphrey Precisely.
Claire (*wondering*) Hmm ... a test of the friendship between our two countries ...?
Jim All I know is, we have to make this deal stick! What happens if it all falls apart now and Kumranistan gets offended?
Claire That wouldn't be good.
Jim It would not! It's a very unstable region. Nuclear proliferation is spreading.
Humphrey Yes. Proliferating, in fact.
Claire (*getting an idea*) Bernard, did the Kumranistan Ambassador return to London after dinner?
Bernard No, he's staying overnight too.

Jim jumps up, energized

Jim The Ambassador! Good idea. Bring him here, right away.
Bernard (*hurrying to the door*) Yes, Prime Minister.

Bernard exits, the door slamming behind him

Jim looks at Claire and Humphrey, then pours himself another Scotch

Jim OK. Here's my question: why didn't MI6 warn us that Aitikeev was a sex addict?
Humphrey Perhaps they don't know.
Jim That's their job, isn't it? We could have been blackmailing Kumranistan for donkeys' years.
Humphrey Please don't say it that way. We don't approve of blackmail as an instrument of government policy.
Jim Since when?
Humphrey Blackmail is criminal, Prime Minister. We use leverage.
Jim (*thinking*) What's this ambassador like?
Humphrey Very good chap. We were undergraduates together at Oxford.
Jim He's a friend?
Humphrey We are friendly.

Jim wanders over to the upstage windows, sighs, mops his brow

Jim So humid.

Claire Clammy. Hope it rains.

The phone rings. They all look at it. Claire gets it, putting her whisky on Jim's desk as she picks up the phone

Hello? ... No, it's Claire Sutton ... (*To Jim*) It's the BBC again ... (*She listens*) I see. Thanks. (*She hangs up*) Piling on the agony. A big new story about global warming has just broken, they're adding that to the Sunday programme too. Global warming computer models have been proved wrong ——

Humphrey How shocking!

Claire The new models show that it's even worse than previously thought. Much more severe. And happening faster.

Jim Is that supposed to be my fault too?

Claire Everything is at the moment. They want to know why the government is dragging its feet on CO2 emission controls.

Jim (*losing it*) Do we have to deal with that tonight, as well as the collapsing conference, the ECB, the BBC, my treacherous cabinet, my disloyal colleagues, your leaks, the illegal immigrant, the run on the pound, the Kumranistani pervert ...? Is there *anything else, anything else* we can pile on me tonight? Oh *yes*! *Global bloody warming*, thank you very much!

Claire It's just that they're going to add it to the catalogue of your failures.

Slowly, Jim turns to look at her

Alleged failures, I mean.

Humphrey May I suggest that you don't worry too much about global warming?

Jim Right. I can't do anything about that tonight, can I?

Humphrey Tell me, why should global warming computer models be any more accurate than financial ones?

Jim What do you mean?

Humphrey Wall Street computer models were designed to prove subprime mortgage derivatives were low risk. These computer models are designed to show global warming is getting worse.

Jim Come off it, Humphrey. All the scientists agree, the evidence is overwhelming.

Humphrey But the hottest year in the twentieth century was nineteen thirty-four.

Claire Haven't you seen that film of the melting icebergs in the Antarctic?

Humphrey Yes. Beautiful, aren't they?

Claire That's caused by CO_2.

Humphrey No, that's caused by warm water masses from the Pacific.

Claire Why are the polar bears becoming extinct?

Humphrey Are they?

Claire The computer models say they are.

Humphrey The people who actually go and count them have found more than there were thirty years ago.

Jim For heaven's sake, Humphrey! If it's all such nonsense why does everyone believe it?

Humphrey (*with a superior chuckle*) Hard to understand, I agree. But some scientists believe it, lots of others want the billions of pounds you can get for research that seems to show that global warming is caused by greenhouse gases, and most of the scientists who disagree can't get published. Journalists love shock-horror stories, governments want to look virtuous to the voters, lefties want a way to bash big oil and it makes all the treehuggers, whale-savers, and everyone at the BBC feel holier than thou and warm and fuzzy inside.

Jim You're saying wind farms don't make sense?

Humphrey (*with even more superior chuckles*) They certainly do, for all the businessmen who are getting enormous government grants for them. But there isn't enough wind to be practical. The total output of all the UK wind turbines put together is less than one quarter of one decent-sized coal-fired power station.

Claire He can't say any of this to the BBC.

Jim Claire, phone them back and give them a version of number six.

Claire Okey-dokey. (*She goes to the phone, and dials*)

Jim I really think you must be misinformed somewhere. Al Gore got the Nobel Peace Prize for his work on global warming.

Humphrey So did Dr Kissinger for his work on the Vietnam War.

Jim has no answer to that

Bernard enters

Claire (*on the phone*) Hello? ... Robin Simpson? ...

Bernard The Ambassador of Kumranistan, Prime Minister.

The Ambassador enters

Claire turns upstage and we don't hear the rest of her phone call

Jim I'm not ready for him. Oh God! (*He turns, and jumps as he sees the*

Ambassador standing right beside him) Oh good!

The Ambassador has a beard, and speaks excellent English. He is wearing silk pyjamas and a monogrammed robe

Jim puts down his whisky on the coffee table and greets the Ambassador like a long-lost friend

Claire hangs up

Jim Ah. Your Excellency!
Ambassador Prime Minister. Please excuse my *déshabillé*, I had just retired for the night when I received your summons.
Jim No problem. (*He loosens his tie*) We're awfully casual at Chequers. Aren't we Bernard?

Bernard takes off his jacket. Jim stares meaningfully at Humphrey

Humphrey?

Humphrey, irritated, pushes his breast pocket handkerchief down, out of sight

Ambassador (*to Humphrey*) Ah, Bubbles, my dear chap.
Jim
Claire   } Bubbles?
Bernard
Ambassador It's like the old days isn't it, late night drinks and all that.
Jim Bubbles?
Ambassador They don't know your old nickname?
Humphrey (*mortified*) No, they ... er ... a silly thing, Prime Minister ... I used to be partial to champagne, that's all.
Jim And this is Claire, Head of the Policy Unit at Number Ten.

Handshakes

Do sit down.

They all sit

I'm glad to hear that you and — Bubbles — are old friends.

Humphrey scowls

Ambassador We are friendly.
Jim So. Bernard's briefed you?
Ambassador Yes indeed.
Jim And?
Ambassador I'm not sure that I know precisely what you're asking
me.
Jim Does Mr Aitikeev mean what he says?
Ambassador Prime Minister, the Foreign Minister consults me on
matters of Kumranistan's policy pertaining to the United Kingdom.
Mr Aitikeev's sexual proclivities are not a matter of public policy.
Jim Did you know about his perverted tastes?
Ambassador I don't consider it my business.
Humphrey Well, unfortunately he's made it your business, wouldn't
you say?
Claire Your Excellency, do you think Mr Aitikeev will renege on his
commitment to the pipeline contract if we cannot — oblige — him
tonight?
Ambassador He can be stubborn.

The Brits exchange glances

Look, I suspect that my personal opinion is the same as yours. But in
my country sex with multiple partners is fine. We allow polygamy.
Jim But this is prostitution.
Ambassador Yes. But I am here, not as a moralist, but as a servant of
our government.
Jim But there are moral considerations here.
Ambassador Indeed there are. And in all fairness to Mr Aitikeev,
I'm quite sure that he did not ask you to obtain virgins for him. (*To
Bernard*) Am I right?

Bernard is wondering if he's losing his sanity

Bernard No, he didn't.
Ambassador As I thought. He'd never do that.
Jim Because?
Ambassador Moral considerations.
Claire Also, wouldn't that be a rather impractical request? Three virgin
call girls?
Ambassador The reason is, he would not defile them. He would want
women who have already been defiled.
Jim That's more moral?
Ambassador In our culture, once a female has been defiled she is

worthless. Dishonoured. Her family will not take her back. If they do, they will kill her. Few men would marry her. Her only real future is in a brothel. As a moral society we have no tolerance for that sort of thing.

Claire Not among women, anyway.

Jim Are you suggesting that we are a less moral society than Kumranistan?

Ambassador (*with irony*) I would say, yes, we are even more rigorous about *purity* than Great Britain. We would certainly not allow page three. Nor some of the publications I saw in a newsagents, like "Lusty Swedish Virgins", or "Big Ones". But in this instance Mr Aitikeev is offering an excellent opportunity to these girls: he's not ungenerous and I'm sure he will give them hundreds of pounds. That's better than death, wouldn't you say?

Claire Yes, but that's not the choice here. In our culture ——

Ambassador Forgive me, but I'm describing our culture. Mr Aitikeev's culture.

Jim But it's unthinkable! There'd be national outrage if it got out! The British people would think this is — just *wrong*!

Ambassador Would they? Maybe they would just be envious.

Jim That's even worse, politically.

Claire British *women* would think it wrong.

Bernard And some men!

Ambassador You say tomayto and I say tomahto.

Jim It's that simple?

Ambassador You believe your values are right. So do we. You believe you should impose your values on us. Many of my people would like to impose their values on you. I say, live and let live.

Claire Are you a Muslim?

Ambassador I'm a diplomat.

Claire Yes, I know, but apart from that what are you?

Ambassador I am a Libra. And a member of the MCC, of course.

Jim
Humphrey } (*doubtfully*) Well that's good ...

Claire You don't want to discuss religion.

Ambassador (*smiling*) Dear me, no. I was brought up to believe it was bad manners to discuss religion in polite company, weren't you?

Jim I think Claire was asking because you seem ... rather English.

Ambassador Harrow and Oxford, Prime Minister. I know how to play a straight bat.

Humphrey Opening bat for Oxford, got a blue.

Ambassador The point is, Prime Minister, my government has expressed a willingness to help you obtain a loan that you need. I shouldn't really be saying this, but it is Mr Aitikeev who really wants this treaty, rather than my government as a whole. Quite frankly, our President is not as pro-Western as Mr Aitikeev and he responds to pressure from our extremists. We have thousands of them in Kumranistan.

Claire How do you define an extremist?

Ambassador Anyone who opposes the government, really.

Jim Well, we've got *millions* of extremists here, actually.

Humphrey (*smirking*) A majority, in fact.

Jim gives him a dirty look

Ambassador The President of Kumranistan, I must warn you, is not convinced by your desire to force what you call democracy down the throats of the peoples of our region when he can see the dismal results of it here.

Jim, angered, stands up. Everyone else stands when he does

Jim You have the nerve to suggest to me that British democracy produces ... dismal results?

Humphrey He didn't mean that. You didn't mean that, did you Freddie?

Ambassador No, no, Prime Minister, I was not referring to you, perish the thought! I mean all those who oppose you, who try to intervene in your noble, tireless work for the British people.

Jim (*after a few moments' consideration*) He's right, actually.

Humphrey Indeed he is.

Jim indicates that everyone should sit down again

Claire Let me try and explain, Your Excellency: procuring women for sex is *against the law* in this country.

Ambassador Of course I know that. But governments break laws whenever they perceive that it's in their national interest. Why do you have the SAS and MI6? What are covert operations, in reality, if not law-breaking operations?

Humphrey We need them. We live in dangerous times.

Ambassador I know. At your level, breaking the odd law doesn't count.

Jim Of course not! So long as the press don't find out. Unless — my God! — what if one of the girls turned out to be underage? That would be ghastly.

Ambassador If you say so. Though many cultures, including my own, allow sex at puberty. In Sweden the age of consent is fifteen.

The Others (*derisively*) Well, Sweden ...

Ambassador In Italy it's only fourteen.
Claire That's different!
Bernard Hot-blooded!
Jim It's the mafia.
Ambassador In Spain it's thirteen.
Jim Is it really?
Claire Never knew that.
Bernard *Awfully* young.
Ambassador And in the Vatican, until recently, it was twelve.
Bernard Twelve??
Ambassador They just raised it to fourteen, to match Italian law.
Jim What kind of law do you call that?
Humphrey The law of supply and demand, I imagine.
Ambassador Not every country is like Britain, you know.
Jim More's the pity.
Ambassador Prime Minister, I urge you to be practical.
Jim It would be the first step on a very slippery slope.
Ambassador Down which you have been sliding, ever since you took
the job. It's the price of power. These girls will get paid. And as a
result unemployment will drop. Oil prices will drop, foreclosures and
repossessions will stop, Greece, Italy and Spain will be bailed out and
Europe will be saved from disaster. (*He walks to the door and turns*)
I bid you good-night.

The Ambassador leaves

Bernard shuts the door and puts on his jacket. Shocked silence

Bernard He's trying to claim some sort of moral equivalence, between
his barbaric culture and ours.
Claire Yes.
Jim There isn't any.
Claire No.
Jim (*thinking*) Is there, Humphrey?

Humphrey gives a noncommittal shrug

I can't possibly agree to this. (*Hopefully*) Can I?
Bernard Of course not!
Jim Claire?
Claire Can't possibly.

Jim is watching Humphrey

Jim Can I, Humphrey?

Humphrey gives another little shrug. Jim is getting no help

   But we have to get this deal, or I'm history.
Humphrey How true.

Nobody knows what to say or how to say it

Bernard So — um — how do you want me to handle Mr Aitikeev's
   request?
Claire Look! Let's discuss this question for what it actually is: is it better
   for three hookers to get screwed than the whole European economy?
Jim If you put it like that, there's no choice.
Claire Quite.
Humphrey Quite.

Black-out

ACT II

SCENE 1

Jim, Humphrey, Claire and Bernard are where they were at the end of Act I. The action is continuous. They are all exceedingly uncomfortable

The act opens with a long silence

Jim (*eventually*) Here's the problem: if we get three prostitutes for him, and it got out somehow, the public wouldn't understand.

Claire No shit!

Jim Is there a way to neutralize that?

Humphrey Prime Minister, you have always taken a very high moral tone. You're on the record against casual sex. If you were now to endorse prostitution as an instrument of policy, there's a chance you could be accused of inconsistency.

Jim There are exceptions to every rule. In this case, I'd make a special exception to allow these girls to have patriotic sex with Aitikeev. They'd be doing this for their country, for Britain! It would actually be an act of the greatest nobility.

Claire In which position?

Bernard Prime Minister, procuring women for sex is a crime.

Jim Mr Aitikeev has diplomatic immunity.

Bernard You haven't!

Jim I could be prosecuted?

Bernard Conspiracy. Pandering.

Jim Only if I knew about it.

Humphrey But you do know about it.

Claire If any of this leaks, he doesn't know. OK?

Jim Do you think people will believe that?

Claire Why not?

Humphrey There are so many things you don't know, what's one more?

Jim gives him a look

Claire We must frame it differently. You called this procuring women for sex, Bernard. We must avoid that kind of inflammatory language, even in a classified document. We can't use the words prostitute, hooker, call-girl or escort. OK? Remember, Clinton got into trouble just for a blow-job.

Humphrey recoils in horror, covering his ears

Humphrey I don't think I wish to be here for this conversation. It is unseemly. (*He goes to the door and turns*) Prime Minister, take no part in this. Deniability works better if there's a *little* truth in it.
Jim But what about these three women?
Humphrey In difficult times, sacrifices do have to be made. Especially by ordinary people.

Humphrey exits

Claire He's right.
Jim Claire, I hear everything you're saying. But — I still have a sort of uncomfortable feeling about this. I know that may sound weird ...
Claire No, I understand ...
Jim Thank you.
Claire Sometimes it's hard for a common sense solution to prevail over ingrained emotional responses, however irrational.
Bernard If we were to go ahead with this, how should it be referred to?
Jim We must make it sound positive. Like the Yanks did with torture — they called it enhanced interrogation techniques.
Claire How about "enhanced entertainment techniques"?
Jim It would have worked, but it's been done.
Bernard (*thinking*) Horizontal diplomacy?
Jim Smoking gun.
Bernard Anglo-Kumranistan Liaison Project?
Jim Bit of a mouthful?
Claire That's it! A euro-job!
Jim Brilliant. A euro-job!
Claire We may need some way to refer to the women, too. What would one call a person who gives a euro-job?
Bernard A eurologist?
Jim What if it *does* get out, how will we defend it?
Bernard No! It's impossible. It's reckless. We're not in London. Mr Aitikeev is staying in this house, not at some hotel. If such a scandal were to get out, we couldn't blame the porter or the concierge for finding the women for him.
Jim There must be somebody to blame. There always is.
Bernard Who?

Jim I don't know, it's your job to find people for me to blame.

Bernard But who? Security is intense. The gates are guarded by the army. Tarts in King's Cross can hardly flag down the royal helicopter. Somebody would have had to authorize it.

Jim Yes, you.

Bernard No, Prime Minister. Not me.

Jim You'd refuse to obey me?

Bernard (*standing at attention*) No sir, you give me a signed instruction and I'll execute it.

Deadlock!

Humphrey knocks at the door and enters

Humphrey The Director-General of the BBC is here to see you.

Jim Why?

Humphrey He says he asked for this meeting last week.

They look at Bernard

Bernard Oh, that's right, Prime Minister. You invited him to pop in for a late drink, he's a neighbour, he lives in Gerrard's Cross actually.

Jim And neither of you thought of cancelling it when this whole Kumranistan thing came up?

Bernard We could hardly have foreseen Mr Aitikeev's unusual request.

Jim But we haven't finished with ... (*speechless with frustration, wracked with indecision*) What does he want?

Humphrey More money, I suppose, that's what the BBC always want.

Jim Money? I suppose we could manage it ... (*An idea! He smiles*) If we brought in the Civil Service Reform Act straightaway.

Humphrey (*instantly on guard*) I would advise against a precipitate approach to the Civil Service Act, Prime Minister, or the BBC, which is a magnificent organization, the Rolls-Royce of broadcasting. It all needs mature deliberation, extensive consultation ——

Jim But if we give more money to the BBC we have to get it from somewhere, Humphrey. If we cut the BBC licence fee it would release more money for the Civil Service. So the Civil Service Act wouldn't be so urgent. What do you think? I know that you love the BBC ...

Humphrey It would seriously ... um ...

Jim ... show everyone that we're serious about putting money back into the voters' pockets. Eh, Humphrey? Good, I'm glad to have your loyal support. Show him in.

Humphrey (*opening the door*) Jeremy. Come in.

Jeremy Burnham, the DG, enters
Humphrey The Director-General, Prime Minister.
Jim Jeremy!
DG Jim!
Jim Drinkie? I'm on Scotch.
DG Fine. Thanks.
Jim I'm afraid we're a bit rushed. Do sit down.

Jim sits the DG down, unceremoniously. Claire brings whiskies for the DG and Jim, and sits. Bernard takes notes

Jim But I'm glad you're here. I'd like to take the opportunity to talk about this TV programme.
DG What programme?
Jim The programme you're running on Sunday, rubbishing me.
DG Are we?
Jim Please, let's not play games.
DG Look — It's um ... not about you specifically, it's — er, it's part of a broad, measured look at the state of the nation.
Jim Rubbishing me, in fact.
DG No, no. Fair. Balanced. Responsible.
Jim Humphrey?
Humphrey Perhaps, Jeremy, you don't realize the full extent of this financial crisis?
Jim Anything that destabilizes Britain at this juncture would be grossly irresponsible.
DG Obviously we don't want to destabilize Britain, as you put it, but we're not the government information service either. We have a duty to reflect all shades of opinion. We are journalists. It's our job to keep the public fully informed. You refused an invitation to appear on it, I understand. That would have ensured that your opinion was represented.
Jim This may come as a big surprise to you, Jeremy, but I don't want to be pre-recorded, edited, quoted out of context and made to look an utter wally.
Humphrey Why don't you postpone this programme at least until the outcome of this Lancaster House Summit is clear?
DG (*putting down his glass*) I hope you're not putting political pressure on the BBC?
Jim Political pressure? Good heavens, no!
Humphrey Most improper. I'm not even political, just a humble civil servant.

Jim And we truly value the independence of the BBC.

DG I'm glad to hear it. But I'm afraid we can't possibly postpone at such short notice, and I can't interfere with content. I'm only the Director-General.

Jim (*as if a great light has dawned*) Oh. I see.

DG The producers would smell a rat. And they'd leak it.

Bernard Um — just to clarify — a rat can leak, but you can't leak a rat.

DG (*irritably*) What?

Bernard A rat ——

Humphrey Thank you, Bernard. Most helpful.

Jim So the BBC's smug and self-satisfied pundits are going ahead with their biased and scurrilous attack on the democratically elected government. Got that, Bernard?

Bernard (*writing*) "... democratically elected government."

DG (*calmly*) No, our team of professional journalists are going ahead with their fair and balanced review of the current political situation. Got that, Bernard?

Bernard nods, still writing

Jim (*standing*) Let me stop you right there. Humphrey has just come up with a really interesting idea. Haven't you, Humphrey?

Humphrey I, er, I ——

Jim He says that in these straitened times making even more cuts in expenditure will be necessary.

DG Impossible. We've already cut to the bone. There's just no more we can do.

Jim Humphrey says that you could sell your digital channels, your websites, BBC Two, Three, Four, Five ... Six, Seven, Eight, Nine ...

Claire All the radio stations ——

Jim — except Radio Four — BBC Publications, BBC Worldwide, the BBC Symphony ——

Claire And the other *three* orchestras ——

Jim — then we could cut the licence fee by eighty per cent. That would be such a relief for you.

DG But Humphrey, you've always said ——

Humphrey I know! I am a great supporter of the BBC, it's just that ——

Jim But you were saying they were overstretched. Weren't you?

Humphrey Well, I, well of course, in normal circumstances, it would, naturally, be an entirely different ball-game, but yes, if the nation's under extreme fiscal and monetary pressure it could be necessary *inter alia* to consider measures which under different economic conditions would not have been desirable but ——

Jim I couldn't have put it better myself. Humphrey pointed out that only about thirty-five to forty-five hours a week on BBC TV is original and distinctive programming. You could get that all on to one channel, easily. That's what Humphrey is proposing, plus one speech radio channel, Radio Four. Aren't you, Humphrey?

Humphrey Well, perhaps the specifics are not so, not so, not so!

Jim So, that's pretty well it. You'd be able to keep all your quality programmes, and the World Service of course, and all your financial worries would be solved.

DG (*standing*) It's a monstrous idea! The BBC is the great bulwark of civilized values against the tide of commercialism, a beacon of world broadcasting.

Jim A beacon of repeats, Hollywood movies, bought-in programmes and bought-in sporting events. Most of what you show on the BBC is no different from what people get on subscription channels, commercial channels, PayTV or sponsorship. That's what you were saying, right, Humphrey?

DG You really can't compare a great public broadcasting service with tacky commercial output.

Jim You can compare the programmes. Cookery programmes, makeovers, quizzes, game shows ——

DG Cultural vandalism!

Jim Why?

DG (*spluttering*) Radio Three ... classical music ...?

Jim (*sweetly reasonable*) Readily available everywhere. You'd be free at last to focus on quality and forget about *The Apprentice*, *The Weakest Link*, *Addicted To Boob Jobs*, *Help! My Dog Is As Fat As Me* and all that junk that so obviously doesn't need to be paid for by the taxpayer.

DG It's quality entertainment.

Jim It's optical chewing gum.

DG But Humphrey ——

Humphrey (*babbling*) Well, you see, Jeremy ... I mean, I yield to no one in my admiration for your, er, you know, I mean, what you say is certainly, at the end of the day, other things being equal, *mutatis mutandis*, in the fullness of time ...

Jim (*sitting*) And then there's the question of your salary.

DG (*sitting*) My salary?

Jim What do you earn now? Six hundred and seventy-five thousand, plus a gigantic expense account.

DG It is a considerably lower salary than the remuneration of many chief executives of comparable corporations.

Claire You poor thing. How ghastly for you.

Jim Anyway, that will all change because running a small organization like the new BBC obviously couldn't command more than about thirty per cent of your current earnings ... but as you've said, it's not about the money, it's about quality and service.

DG Thirty per cent?

Jim You'd still be earning a lot more than me! Or even Humphrey. Nothing to complain about there.

DG The cabinet would never back you on this.

Jim Actually, that's one thing they'd definitely back me on. When we go on the BBC your presenters just jeer and sneer at all of us. Posturing opportunists who've never had to take responsibility for anything, following their party line.

DG (*emphatically*) The BBC reports facts and reflects opinions but it does not have any editorial policy.

Jim Maybe, maybe not. But it has a pretty consistent view on a whole lot of issues: immigration, multiculturalism, global warming, joining the euro ... Anyway, we'll study your comments on this but I think Humphrey's basic idea is pretty sound. So — (*he stands up*) — I'll wait to hear from you.

DG You certainly will.

Bernard puts away his notepad and pen

Jim Incidentally, to change the subject, if I were to give a live interview in that programme on Sunday, from Chequers ——

Humphrey Live? Are you quite sure, Prime Minister?

Jim Yes. So they can't edit what I say. I would feel that the BBC was at least trying to be fair. Especially if the interview was the last item, so that I could answer all the points ...

DG (*thinking as he speaks*) I don't see why we can't manage that. I'll have a word.

Jim Rather a scoop, really.

DG (*doubtfully*) Yes. It might be.

Jim It *would* be! Thank you for your time.

DG Thank you, Prime Minister.

Bernard shows the DG out and shuts the door

The DG has left his unfinished whisky on the coffee table

Jim He won't cancel the programme, but they'll give me the live interview at the end of it.

Humphrey Live? I do admire your courage, Prime Minister.
Jim Oh God! Have I been courageous?

They all nod

Humphrey, help me! What will I say?
Humphrey Goodbye?
Claire At least the Prime Minister's bought us some time.
Bernard Time for what?
Claire Time to think of something to say to the BBC. And something to keep Mr Aitikeev in this deal! (*She looks at her watch*) Talking of which, Jim, it's getting pretty late. If we're going to find three call girls for Aitikeev we have to get on with it.
Jim Is there *no* other way?
Claire We could just say no to him.
Jim Can't risk that. Collapse of conference, collapse of backbench support, collapse of coalition, collapse of cabinet, collapse of my career! This is the biggest disaster since Dunkirk.
Humphrey I think not, Prime Minister.
Jim Name a bigger one.
Humphrey The Freedom of Information Act.
Jim Humphrey, I'm begging you, what is your advice?
Humphrey Well, Prime Minister ... one hesitates to say this but there are times when circumstances conspire to create an inauspicious concatenation of events that necessitate a metamorphosis, as it were, of the situation such that what happened in the first instance to be of primary import fraught with hazard and menace can be relegated to a secondary or indeed tertiary position while a new and hitherto unforeseen or unappreciated element can and indeed should be introduced to support and supercede those prior concerns not by confronting them but by subordinating them to the over-arching imperatives and increased urgency of the previously unrealized predicament which may in fact, *ceteris paribus*, now only be susceptible to radical and remedial action such that you might feel forced to consider the currently intractable position in which you find yourself.

Jim is nonplussed

Jim What does he mean, Bernard?
Bernard I um — I uh think that he's perhaps suggesting the possibility that you, um consider your position. Resign, in fact, Prime Minister.
Jim I'm not resigning, Humphrey. And you can consider the Civil Service Reform Act a done deal. So there!

A tense silence. Jim sits heavily and puts his head in his hands
Jim What about Mr Aitikeev? What would the Americans do?
Bernard Shall we ask them?
Jim Not the White House.
Claire How about the CIA? I know somebody at the sharp end. (*She goes to the phone and dials. Flirting*) Yes, hi, it's Claire Sutton ... I'm at Chequers, actually. Fine, but we have a problem and I wondered if you had a view, or any suggestions ... Here's the thing: the conference here has been going fine till now ... everyone's ready to agree — yes, incredible! I know. But now, unfortunately, Mr Aitikeev ... yes, the little Kumranistan Foreign Minister, he's demanding that we get him three escorts tonight to have sex with ... Yes, an orgy ... Yes, tricky, any thoughts? ... We don't have people who do that.
Jim Do what?

She mimes shooting a gun. Jim, Humphrey and Bernard look at her in horror

Ring off!
Humphrey I'm leaving again!

Humphrey hurries out, with his hands over his ears

Jim Good.

The door closes loudly behind Humphrey

Claire (*coolly, on the phone*) No, that won't fly here ... You think that might help?
Jim Get off that phone. Murdoch might have hacked it!
Claire Any other thoughts? ... I don't know, it's after ten p.m. here and we don't keep a vicar on the premises ——
Jim NOW!
Claire Sorry, got to rush, the PM is calling me. Call you later. (*She hangs up*)

Jim is horrified

Jim Assassination? Is that what he suggested?
Claire I agree, it's not practical.
Jim It's impractical *and immoral*! We can't just go around murdering the leaders of democratically elected foreign governments?

Bernard We have actually facilitated the Americans in this sort of operation, I believe.

Jim We've never done it ourselves!

Claire Maybe ... you know, maybe we *should* consider it, if it's what the people want.

Bernard Which people?

Jim Our people! I am their leader, I must follow them. That's how democracy's *defined*: giving the British people what they want. Don't you know anything?

Bernard Aitikeev was elected too. You're saying our democracy trumps everyone else's?

Jim Obviously!!

Bernard And how would we know if that's what our people want, they haven't been asked?

Jim (*exasperated*) It's perfectly simple, Bernard! They elected me. I represent the will of the people. If I want it, they do.

Claire Right. It's pretty obvious they don't want us to be held to ransom by little perverts like Aitikeev.

Jim But we can't assassinate him — it's unthinkable, it's wrong... it's corrupt ... how would we do it, actually?

Claire It's not practical, we don't have the people to do that sort of thing.

Jim Are you sure?

Claire No, but I'm sure we don't have them here, tonight. Besides which, he's here, at Chequers. Even PC Plod could work out we were involved. But we could ask the White House to send a drone.

Jim A drone?

Claire They're sending them all over the place now.

Bernard They're not very selective. It might kill *us*!

Claire We could indicate Mr Aitikeev's bedroom window and ask them to be careful.

Jim It would be obvious that we did it.

Claire Could we say it was Al-Qaeda?

Jim How would it make our security people feel? No!

Bernard Um — what was that you said about a vicar?

Claire He suggested getting some religious input.

Jim Why do the Yanks bring God into everything?

Claire He's on their side, isn't he?

Jim So what did he suggest?

Claire Pray. (*She sniggers*)

Bernard Murder, and prayer?

Claire That's the way they do things.

Bernard Aren't Americans odd?

Jim Maybe it's not such a bad idea.
Claire What?
Jim Prayer.
Claire Are you kidding me?
Jim Why not? Bush and Blair used to pray.
Claire Look what happened to the rest of us!

Jim kneels. He points to the floor

Jim Bernard!

Bernard kneels, uncertainly. Jim and he close their eyes and clasp their hands in prayer. Claire watches them, pityingly. After a moment, Jim opens his eyes

Wait. I need to think for a moment. I've never had to ask God's advice about whether or not to supply a trio of prostitutes before! He might be offended.
Bernard Not with you, surely. Aitikeev is the sinner here.
Jim That's right. If God gives me the OK, then it can't be a sin. And if He says no, I won't do it. So I'm in the clear, either way.
Bernard But ... I wouldn't use profane language to God, if I were you.

Jim stares coldly at him

You know, like the eff word — (*he whispers*) — don't actually say that Aitikeev wants to eff three hookers.
Jim (*icily*) Thank you for those helpful comments, Bernard.
Bernard I'm just saying that wouldn't be the norm, that's all.
Claire Bernard, I imagine God knows all the four letter words, in every language. He's supposed to be omniscient.
Jim Right. In which case ... (*realizing*) ... He would know about all this already. In fact, He could be waiting to hear from me.
Claire Then I shouldn't keep Him waiting too long, if I were you. He's probably got a lot of other stuff to deal with.
Jim (*on his dignity*) OK, but I am Prime Minister of the United Kingdom of Great Britain and Northern Ireland *and* one of the Presidents of the European Union. I think He knows He has to find time for me when I need it.
Bernard I'm sure He does, Prime Minister.
Claire We'll see, won't we?
Jim Come on, Claire! You too. Come on. (*He taps the floor beside him*)

Reluctantly Claire kneels

O God, our rock in ages past ... Sorry I've been out of touch for a bit.
We're all down here at Chequers — as you know already, of course,
being omniscient — ready to sign a pipeline contract that could
save the EU from imploding. And now, out of the clear blue sky, Mr
Aitikeev has demanded etcetera etcetera you *know* it all ... so if we
don't get him um three call girls — excuse my language, Lord, I'm
trying to find a nice way to put it — he'll renege, the conference will
collapse and the opportunity for agreement and harmony and peace
on earth — well, in Europe anyway — will be lost. So my question is:
which is the greater evil, O Lord? Is it really OK for me to authorize
procuring some little scrubbers for him to have sex with? I'm having
trouble squaring that away. And oh, and by the way, if you do tell me
to get him these girls, what do we do with them afterwards? Give
them an honour? Or hand them over to the CIA to send to one of those
prisons in Poland that don't exist anymore? I look forward to hearing
from you at your earliest convenience. Amen.
Bernard Amen.

The other two look at Jim

Jim How was that?
Bernard Clear, respectful.
Claire Now what?
Jim See if He answers.

*LIGHTNING! THUNDER! There is a huge flash of lightning outside the
windows, and a loud crack of thunder, followed by sudden rain beating
against the windows. Bernard crosses to the window, on his knees*

Bernard Maybe that's it!
Claire Don't be silly, a thunderstorm's been forecast since yesterday.
Jim If it is God, he sounds angry.
Bernard (*standing*) Obviously! Procuring prostitutes? No way he'll
approve.

More tremendous lightning and thunder

See?
Claire (*smiling*) People have been turned into pillars of salt for less.
Jim Claire, this is a serious problem!

Claire I agree! So let's find a serious way of tackling it!

Jim We're trying prayer, since we have no other ideas. OK?

Claire OK. Is God telling you to get party girls for Mr Aitikeev, or not?

Jim walks to the upstage window and peers out, waiting for an answer. There is no more lightning, but some distant rumbles of thunder

Jim I think what He's saying is: search your heart and find a way to do what's right.

Claire That sounds like *just* the sort of thing he'd say.

Distant thunder. Jim looks out. Does the sky have more to impart? He waits. There is a final flicker of distant lightning and crack of thunder!

Jim You know what? I see a way out of this hideous dilemma. (*Suddenly he's a believer!*) Thank you, God!

Claire Are you all right?

Jim God's given me an inspiration! I've been trying to think how I could justify doing this for Aitikeev and I couldn't find a way. It's just plain wrong, no matter which way you look at it.

Bernard So ...?

Jim Why must they be British girls?

Bernard What?

Jim Every time I have a meeting with the Women and Equality Unit or Justice For Women, they tell me there's a huge problem in our major cities with sex trafficking. Foreign girls, brought to London by the lorry load, some of them swindled into coming to the UK for a job, lent money for travel, put in massage brothels and kept there until they repay the money — if ever! So ...?

Claire (*softly, delighted*) I see!! Get them!

Jim No family here. No one'll miss them! Probably don't even speak English. Yeah, that's it! — we get ones that can't speak English. Then there's no way they can tell anyone anything. We give them to Aitikeev tonight, deport them tomorrow. It's done.

Claire No one would ever know. That's perfect!

Bernard How is that perfect? What about human rights?

Jim We can't protect *everybody*, Bernard! We protect our citizens. What's the matter with you?

Claire It's collateral damage, that's all.

Bernard Weren't you asking God for moral guidance?

Claire I share Bernard's doubts about that.

Jim looks at her, surprised

I wouldn't give God the credit. It's your idea, Jim, and it's brilliant.
Bernard No! We'd be sex slave traffickers ourselves.
Jim (*with crocodile tears*) Bernard, if some illegal immigrants have sex with Aitikeev, I'm sorry about it but if they're not British, they're not my problem.
Claire Bernard, you really are being a little sentimental.

Bernard stares at them, puzzled

Jim And none of this is *my fault*! You want to blame somebody, go talk to Aitikeev. But no, you won't do that. So come up with a better plan or shut up and get it done!
Bernard I do not believe that women are worthless.
Jim What?
Claire When did Jim say that?
Jim I don't think women are worthless. It was foreigners I was talking about.
Bernard It seemed to me to be the implication of the whole discussion, of everything the Ambassador said. And I personally am most reluctant to break the law and procure three women for what seems to me an immoral purpose.
Jim Immoral? The future of Europe is at stake, the money supply, mass unemployment ...?
Bernard I just think it's not right. This is a moral dilemma that I really don't know how to address. (*He goes to sit in another part of the room*)
Jim Bernard, ever since this started you've been bleating on about whether or not something's "right"! We're politicians, not bishops. We're not here to do what's right, we're here to serve the public.
Claire It's not easy, I understand that.
Bernard What if we do get this deal signed? What if the Prime Minister loses the next election and the next government has a different policy?
Claire There are no guarantees.
Bernard And for no guarantees I'm to be an accomplice in a euro-job?
Jim The deal will stick. It will be a treaty. Great Britain will be a signatory and we always keep our word.
Claire We don't, actually.
Jim Well, we often do. And we definitely would in this case.
Claire (*crossing to the phone*) Fine. Bernard, *I'll* organize it before it

gets any later.

Jim refills his whisky glass, which he has held on to since the DG scene

Who do I phone?
Bernard To get the helicopter?
Claire To get three young ladies.
Bernard You don't know?
Claire No. How would I know?
Bernard *So how do you think I know?*
Jim Let me get this straight. We've finally decided to do this *and you don't even know how?*
Claire Do *you* know how?
Jim *(losing it)* I can't believe this! The TV news shows tell me we're crawling with illegal foreign hookers, and nobody even knows how to *find* one? What is going *on* here?
Bernard Try the Vice Squad. They'll know.
Jim *(yelling)* You want to call the Vice Squad — and ask them to find three prostitutes — and put them on the royal helicopter? Have you lost your mind? Banner fucking headlines!

A dog barks outside. Claire crosses to a window, looks out at something, looks back at Jim

Claire I'm just popping out. Back in a minute.

Claire goes out. Then we see her pass the window, under an umbrella

Jim What's that about?
Bernard Don't know. *(He peers out of the window)* She seems to be talking to somebody out there.
Jim Who?
Bernard Can't really see. Trees are in the way.

Jim turns away, shaking his head, despairing

Jim So. We're stuck. *(He sits on the sofa)*

Bernard sits beside him. A moment of calm

Bernard Aren't you worried that this is wrong, Prime Minister?
Jim It seems to be necessary, Bernard. Government is seldom about right or wrong. It's about choosing the lesser evil.

Bernard (*stubbornly*) It can be about right or wrong.

Jim (*gently*) Are you sure you're in the right job? I can always arrange a transfer, you know. To the Archbishop of Canterbury, for instance.

Bernard You want to get rid of me?

Jim Not get rid of you, Bernard. A sideways move, find you a good home. Meanwhile, we have a crisis.

Bernard A moral crisis?

Jim A *survival* crisis, which is much more serious. *And* a moral crisis. I have to survive this weekend and stay in office. If I don't, I can't do the things that the people elected me to do: the health service, schools and all that crap. I have a moral obligation to do whatever is necessary to stay in power.

Bernard I'm not sure that the end justifies the means. Look where that philosophy leads: Stalin wanted all the farms in the Ukraine collectivized. He thought there'd be more food. The peasant farmers opposed him, so he ordered all five million of them to be killed.

Jim Actually, if you kill five million people there *is* more food.

Bernard Does that make it right?

Jim Depends on whether or not you're one of the five million.

Claire enters, in wellies and holding a dripping umbrella

Where did you go?

Claire I heard a dog bark out there. I recognized it. It belongs to the cook. The illegal immigrant cook, remember?

Jim Oh God!! (*He is not praying!*) I forgot about the *cook*! What are we doing about that?!

Bernard Claire, really! We have more pressing matters tonight.

Claire That was the cook's daughter out there, walking the dog. Her eighteen-year-old daughter.

Slowly, in unison, Jim and Bernard rise from the sofa, staring at her, stunned

Jim Are you suggesting ...?

Claire Yes. I know there's only one of her. But she's very attractive. And it would show Aitikeev that we're trying.

Jim Would it?

Claire And she's not a virgin. She's had sex, more than once.

Bernard How on earth do you know?

Claire I asked her.

Bernard And she just ... told you?

Claire nods

Jim But ... but ...

Claire An illegal immigrant. Exactly what you wanted.

Jim But the daughter of a member of our staff here ... did you tell her what we want her to do?

Claire I sort of hinted at it.

Jim What precisely did you hint?

Bernard A hint can't be precise, Prime Minister, because by definition —

Jim *Bernard*!

Claire Sex with a very rich and powerful man. She seems interested.

Jim It's for Britain, right? It's the right thing to do, right?

Claire Jim, you were the one who said it would be patriotic. "An act of the greatest nobility," you said.

Jim She's a foreigner, it can't be patriotic for her.

Claire It will be when her papers come through. You're giving her a chance to serve her new country.

Bernard (*thinking it through*) An act of retrospective patriotism.

Jim Shut up, Bernard! Claire, the answer is —

Bernard "PRIME MINISTER PIMPS HIS COOK'S DAUGHTER FOR SEX WITH FOREIGN DIPLOMAT AT CHEQUERS!"

Jim No. I just can't go through with it. Her mother's a member of my staff.

Claire OK. (*She shrugs and turns to go*)

Bernard Claire! Wait! What if the girl tells her mother?

Claire I took care of that. I asked her if she'd ever heard of the Immigration Detention Centre at Harmondsworth.

Bernard Had she?

Claire Of course, it's like asking if she'd heard of Guantanamo. I told her "If you ever tell anyone about this, including your mother, that's where you'll end up." I couldn't threaten anything worse. I'll go and tell the girl it's off for tonight.

Claire exits

Jim's anxiety has been building. It is reaching a high level. He pours himself another stiff drink

Jim Phone the Home Secretary. Get citizenship for the cook.

Bernard Why?

Jim Because ... what if she does tell her mother?

Bernard Hopefully she won't.

Jim But if she does? How would the mother react?

Bernard Probably ... not awfully well. How would you react if you were her mother?

Jim You know ... I wonder if I might be pleased.

He pours all of the five unfinished tumblers of Scotch (four on the coffee table and one on the side table) into the glass in his hand, starting from centre stage and moving to stage right

It would give me the leverage to get a work permit.

Bernard How many drinks have you had, Prime Minister?

Jim (*holding up the one glass which now has all the whisky in it*) Just the one. (*He drinks*)

Claire comes in, holding her wellies. She puts her shoes back on

Claire OK. She's gone.

Jim Thank God!

Bernard To get the cook a work permit she needs to have special skills.

Jim She makes great dumplings, I don't bloody care!! Phone the Home Secretary now!

Bernard (*glancing at his watch*) Now?

Jim Yes, NOW, DAMMIT!!

Bernard crosses to the phone and dials

Bernard Ah, hello. Um — sorry to wake you, Home Secretary ... Oh, you're just having a nightcap? Good. The PM asked me to call you about the cook at Chequers ... the cook ... I know it's nearly midnight but we've found out she's an illegal immigrant, and he wants her to be given a UK visa immediately ... I think, because the PM likes her dumplings ... No, that's not a sexist remark, Home Secretary ... I see, thank you, bye. (*He rings off*) So sorry, Prime Minister, I think the Home Secretary's had a few, it's never any use trying to talk to her after six p.m.

Claire Do you think we'd better let the Ambassador know that we can't get any girls for Aitikeev?

Jim Yes. Go and get him.

Bernard exits

The phone rings

Claire! Get the phone!

Claire answers the phone

Claire Yes? ... Who? ... Oh yes. We all loved your goulash and dumplings this evening ...

Jim backs away in horror, whimpering
Yes ... Yes ... I'll phone you back. (*She hangs up*) The cook's daughter has talked to her mother.
Jim Already?
Claire The cook wants to talk to you, Jim.

They stare at each other, paralyzed by indecision. The phone rings again. They both back away from it

Jim I'm not answering it. You get it!
Claire I don't know what to say!!
Jim Just get it!!! You started it. It's your fault!!

Claire is cracking up

Bernard enters

Bernard The Ambassador's coming. (*He sees their catatonic state, and cautiously answers the phone*) Yes ...?

Humphrey enters

Yes? ... My God! ... and where did you get this? ... Of course I deny it. Yes. There is absolutely no foundation at all for that story ... of course you can't quote me, I'm not going dignify that rubbish with a comment. (*He hangs up*)

They are all staring at him

It seems that the cook has talked to the *Daily Mail*.
Humphrey What about?
Claire She only just phoned here.
Bernard Well, she just phoned there too.
Jim Oh — my — God!!!
Humphrey What's the problem?
Claire (*ignoring him*) Can we buy them off with a promise of some

future policy scoop?

Jim 'Course not, it's a newspaper. They're interested in sex, not government!

Claire Jim, I think you'd better talk to the cook? We have to stop it going any further.

Humphrey Stop *what* going any further?

Jim I can't possibly.

Claire She was very insistent.

Jim I don't talk to ordinary people unless there's an election going on.

Claire If you don't, goodness knows what she'll ——

Jim Just phone her back and ask her just what the bloody hell she wants!

Bernard takes a deep breath, then dials

Humphrey What is all this *about*?

Bernard (*on the phone*) Yes, it's the Prime Minister's Principal Private Secretary here. Unfortunately he is too busy to talk to you, so can you please tell me what it is you want? ... I see ... I see ... I see ...

With each "I see" his voice gets gloomier and gloomier

I see. (*He hangs up*) She's discovered the newspapers will give her cash ... if her daughter will tell what happened tonight in her own words.

Humphrey Which are ...?

Bernard Um ... that some woman approached her in the garden and asked her to have sex ... with you, Prime Minister.

Jim With *me*?!

Humphrey Is that true?

Jim No of course it's not!! (*He advances angrily on Bernard*)

Bernard I'm just telling you what she ——

Jim (*grabbing Bernard by the lapels*) It's an outrageous lie!

Bernard (*breaking Jim's grip*) I am merely the messenger! (*He points at Claire*) It was her idea! I knew it would be disastrous.

Claire How much does she want?

Bernard I don't know, I forgot to ask. (*He straightens his jacket and tie*)

Humphrey Prime Minister. I think I understand what's been going on here and I have an idea. I know how to deal with this? May I?

Jim (*heartfelt*) Yes! *Please*!

Humphrey leaves. Bernard, scowling at Claire, sits and sulks

Claire We have to stop this going public.
Bernard Oh, brilliant! Got any more bright ideas?

Jim is nearly at the end of his tether. Claire is thinking

Claire Look. As far as the *Mail* knows, it could be a scam. If we deny
it and they still run the story, we slap a libel writ on them and clean up
financially. And deport her.
Jim Yes, she's not important in the great scheme of things.
Bernard Who is?
Jim Well — *I* am, actually! What's our story going to be, when the press
talk to us?
Claire We say we can't talk about it. National security.
Jim How do we describe procuring sex with the cook's daughter as
national security?
Claire We don't talk about that!
Jim That's what the papers will want to talk about!
Claire For God's sake, Jim! You don't give journalists what they want,
it only encourages them!
Jim (*in abject terror*) Oh my God! Oh my God! Oh my God! What am I
going to do, what am I going to do? (*In utter despair, he crawls under
his desk and curls up in a foetal position*) What do we do? We can't
ignore the facts.
Bernard If you can't ignore facts you have no business being in
government.

Humphrey enters, smiling

*He can't see Jim. As he turns to go, he notices Jim under the desk. He
approaches the desk and knocks on the table top*

Humphrey Prime Minister?
Jim Fuck off.
Humphrey It's done. The cook and her daughter were upstairs in their
accommodation. At your request the Diplomatic Protection Group has
taken them into protective custody and is turning them over to the
Ministry of Defence Police.
Jim My request?
Humphrey I requested it on your behalf, Prime Minister. The MoD
Police have complete police jurisdiction over the entire UK. They
have the power to arrest, detain, and then place a Control Order upon
anyone at all.

Jim (*coming out from under the desk*) How would a Control Order work?

Humphrey House arrest, usually. Plus no access to mobile phones, the internet or the media — wherever they believe that lives may be saved or injuries prevented by so doing. Lasts for up to a year, and in practice is infinitely renewable.

Jim Fine. Impose a Control Order.

Humphrey The Home Secretary has to do that.

Jim Oh, not her!

Humphrey With the approval of the High Court.

Jim Who says?

Humphrey The European Convention on Human Rights.

Jim Bloody Europe again! Taking away our rights.

Bernard Well actually, Prime Minister, taking away your rights but increasing everybody else's.

Jim So they're entitled to a trial? That's not fair!

Humphrey Yes but, broadly speaking, a trial can be held in secret, the judge can't quash the control order unless it's "obviously flawed". And the evidence against them is never really challenged.

Claire Why?

Humphrey Because it's withheld from them and their lawyers.

Jim Oh that's good!

Claire But we still have to make a deal with the Home Secretary.

Bernard I can try to get her private secretary to bounce it past her one evening when she's had a few.

Jim And if that doesn't work?

Humphrey We could leak that the Home Secretary allowed an illegal immigrant slash suspected terrorist to get into the country and infiltrate Chequers. Yes. Drunk in charge of the Home Office. That should do it.

Jim Brilliant! She'll cooperate.

Humphrey At this point, the MoD police just need an allegation: are you prepared to state that the cook and her daughter are, in fact, terrorists?

Jim Me?

Humphrey Yes, because no judge will want to declare your allegation "obviously flawed". You are the Prime Minister, Prime Minister.

Jim Yes I am! And I am prepared to state the following. Categorically. Um ... I ... um ... (*Out of ideas, he turns to Bernard*)

Bernard Prime Minister, I think you are prepared to state to the police that both the cook and her daughter are in possession of information that, if it were known, could lead to a rapid escalation of violence leading to the loss of thousands more lives in the ongoing war.

Jim Yes I am. (*Relieved*) That's actually even true! Make a note of what you just said. (*To Humphrey*) I'll sign it in the morning.
Humphrey Excellent decision, Prime Minister. (*He heads for the door*)

There is a knock on the door. Humphrey stops

Bernard The Ambassador.

Jim loosens his tie and sits on the sofa. Bernard takes off his jacket. Humphrey pushes his breast pocket handkerchief out of sight again, then opens the door. The Ambassador is standing there

Humphrey Freddie, the Prime Minister is expecting you.

The Ambassador enters

Ambassador Thank you.
Humphrey The Kumranistan Ambassador, Prime Minister.
Jim Yes, come in. Do sit down.
Ambassador Thank you, Prime Minister.

Humphrey exits, closing the door

Jim I'm not going to beat about the bush. I'm afraid you'll have to tell Mr Aitikeev that we haven't been able to find a suitable ... candidate.
Ambassador He's guessed that by now, Prime Minister. I'm afraid that half an hour ago, he informed our President that he does not find you sympathetic to our national aspirations. The pipeline deal is, I'm afraid, no more.
Jim Oh? Really? Then tell your Mr Aitikeev that if he withdraws from this pipeline agreement, all those weapons systems we sold you will be cancelled forthwith.
Ambassador But we have them already, Prime Minister.
Jim (*surprised*) Have you? Then we'll stop supplying the spare parts. They'll be useless within months. Full of sand. Probably are already.
Ambassador It won't matter, Prime Minister. We are making a new weapons agreement with the Russians.
Jim You are? You may go.

The Ambassador goes to the door and opens it

And please inform Mr Aitikeev that Great Britain is breaking off diplomatic relations with your country.

Ambassador (*shocked*) Are you serious?
Jim I am. I'm giving you forty-eight hours to get to Heathrow.
Ambassador What do you think I am? A snail?

The Ambassador walks out

Bernard hurries to shut the door

Bernard Was that wise, Prime Minister?
Jim I don't know and I no longer care!
Bernard I think I lost my moral compass tonight. I can tell you one
   thing: this incident will not be in my memoirs. (*He sits*)
Claire Of course not. Memoirs are not the truth, they're the case for
   the defence.
Jim I think Humphrey's right. It's all over! (*He sighs a deep and
   heartfelt sigh*) Bernard, tomorrow morning, arrange for me to see the
   Queen and offer my resignation.
Bernard I'm so sorry, Prime Minister.

*Jim nods, hopelessly. Suddenly, there is another huge flash of lightning
and a thunder-clap. The Lights flicker and go out*

Jim Oh God!

*Humphrey enters, opening both double doors for the first time in the
play, seen in majestic silhouette as if on a cross*

Humphrey No, Prime Minister, just me. I have returned with the answer
   to all your problems.

The Lights flicker back on as he closes the doors

   Global warming!
Jim What?
Bernard He said "Global warming", Prime Mini ——
Jim I heard what he said! What does he mean? (*To Humphrey*) I thought
   you were against it.
Humphrey Everyone's against it, Prime Minister. I suddenly realized,
   that's the beauty of it! We can get a unanimous agreement with our
   European partners to do something about it.
Jim How can we do something about something that isn't happening?
Humphrey Much easier to solve an imaginary problem than a real one.
   If everyone thinks global warming's real, they'll all want to stop it as

long as it doesn't cost too much.

Jim Do you believe it's real?

Humphrey Do you?

Jim I don't know.

Humphrey Nor do I. Haven't the faintest idea. But it doesn't matter what we think. The question now is, what are we going to do about it?

Jim If it isn't happening, what can we do about it?

Humphrey There's so much we can do: impose taxes, stiffen European rules about carbon emissions and rubbish disposal, make massive investments in wind turbines ... we can agree, in fact, under your leadership, to save the world.

Jim I like that.

Claire But Russia, India, China, Brazil ... they'll never cooperate.

Humphrey They won't have to. We simply ask them to agree to review their emissions policies.

Jim And will they?

Humphrey Of course. And they'll decide not to change them. Meanwhile you can talk about the future of the planet, look states-manlike, and it will be fifty years before anybody could possibly prove you were wrong.

Bernard You can explain away anything you've said previously by saying the computer models were flawed ...

Jim The voters will love me.

Claire (*warning*) But you'll have more government expenditure.

Jim Yes, how would we pay for it? We're broke.

Humphrey Raise a special global warming tax on fuel now. But phase in expenditure gradually, over the next fifty years ...

Jim That would get us out of the hole now ...

Claire And our allies ...

Humphrey That's all we need.

Jim Everyone benefits! Conservation ... reducing dependence on foreign oil ... a face-saving excuse to abandon the pipeline ...

Claire The Germans will be pleased, they have a big green movement.

Bernard We can even get the Frogs on board as long as they get more benefits than anyone else ...

Jim OK. My broadcast is Sunday morning. You've got today to get the conference to agree.

Humphrey That's not a problem. They'll be desperate to announce something when they get home.

Bernard There is one problem ... Nothing will have actually been achieved.

Humphrey It will sound as though it has. And people will think it has.

Jim That's all that matters.

Black-out

SCENE 2

Jim is at his desk. A Union Jack and a European Union flag are displayed behind him

Simon Chester, a BBC interviewer, is facing him across the desk. There are digital cameras on Jim and Simon. The audience sees the output on monitors all over the theatre. Humphrey and Bernard are watching the onstage TV set

Simon (*talking to the camera*) So, to summarize, there is a deepening financial crisis, division in the cabinet, opinion polls are at their lowest for seven years, government borrowing at an all-time high and apparently no agreement on what to do about it all at the Lancaster House conference. Today's papers are asking if Jim Hacker's government can survive. I'm here in Chequers, live, with the Prime Minister. (*He turns to Jim*) Can you survive, Prime Minister?

Jim Of course. All governments go through difficult patches and ——

Simon (*interrupting*) Yes, but this is more than just a difficult patch, isn't it?

Jim It's a world problem, it obviously has repercussions on the UK but we ——

Simon (*interrupting*) But it is worse here than lots of other countries, isn't it?

As Simon speaks, Humphrey opens the doors to admit Claire, who hurries into the shot and hands a red box to Jim

Jim Would you excuse me? I've been waiting for this. (*He opens the box and pulls out a folder*) I think you'll find this puts a very different complexion on things. It is perhaps the most momentous document you'll ever see.

Simon May we know what it is?

Jim It's the final communiqué from the conference: a binding agreement on all members of the European Union to devote unprecedented sums to the battle against global warming. You saw the latest IPCC report? That the situation is not only far more serious than we thought but also deteriorating far more quickly.

Simon Yes, that was one of the things I was coming to, but if we could talk first about the level of debt ——

Jim I obviously haven't made myself clear. I'm not talking about day-to-day issues, I'm talking about the survival of life on this planet. I do realize that you have to try and score your political points. That's your job. But the new findings on global warming make all other issues insignificant.

Simon You can't call our debt level insignificant ——

Jim Look, Simon, you can chase all the little preoccupations of daily journalism. As Prime Minister, I have to look to the future of our country and the world. Not tomorrow's headlines but ten, twenty, fifty years ahead. (*Churchillian*) A heavy responsibility.

Simon is astounded. Jim returns to his own voice

This document is so momentous, it commits Europe to an investment of five trillion euros to stop global warming.

Simon How can we possibly afford to spend that sum of money?

Jim We can't afford not to.

Simon But if the money's not there ——

Jim We are faced with a catastrophic rise in sea levels. Torrential storms. Melting ice caps. Widespread hunger. Mass migrations.

Simon Are you sure?

Jim Computer models don't lie. They have no ulterior motive.

Simon But five trillion euros ——

Jim Over time. In the early years it will be less, of course. We have much research to do on ... (*using his reading glasses, he cribs from the folder*) ... carbon sequestration plants, new fast-breeder reactors, biofuels ...

Simon Even so, surely taxes will have to go up. People won't like that.

Jim Simon, people aren't as selfish as you think they are. (*Gently, to the camera*) They are worried about their children, their grandchildren, the future of mankind. If it means doing without a gasguzzler or a fourth plasma TV set, that's a sacrifice most people are willing to make.

Simon Prime Minister, I did want to talk to you about Cabinet divisions ...

Jim There's no cabinet division on the survival of our species. My cabinet will support the prospect of all this investment in twenty years' time.

Simon They won't be in office then.

Jim I think that's an unworthy remark. Are you saying that a government can't make commitments beyond the immediate future?

Simon No, but twenty years?

Jim We are looking at a historic consensus. The agreement of every single country in the European Union. (*Churchillian*) It will stand alongside Magna Carta and the American Declaration of Independence.

Simon OK. To move on quickly ——

Jim And if I might just strike a personal note. (*To the camera*) I would like to say how humble it makes me to think that I, as President of the Commission, was able to bring about this historic agreement which, quite frankly, transcends any achievement of any post-war government. It is, as I say, humbling. Deeply humbling.

Simon Thank you, Prime Minister. (*To the camera*) And there we have to leave it. Until next week, goodbye.

The screens go blank. Applause from Humphrey, Bernard and Claire

Jim Well, Simon, you certainly know how to do a tough interview.

Simon Thank you, Prime Minister.

Simon walks out, a defeated man

Bernard and Claire produce champagne and glasses, open it and pour

Humphrey Magnificent, Prime Minister.

Claire I think you got away with it, Jim. But the cabinet will have been pretty surprised, we'll have to square them fast. Also, I've been in touch with some press agents ——

Jim Bob Geldof?

Claire Can't reach him, but we're waiting to hear from Bono.

Jim OK.

Claire And I just got a text from Angelina Jolie and Brad Pitt! They will endorse this!

Jim is triumphant, ecstatic

Jim That's it! That's all we need! Cabinet will never go against them. I'm back.

Bernard Claire, give me their contact details and I'll get them to a dinner at Number Ten.

Jim offers a glass of champagne to Humphrey

Jim Bubbles.

Claire (*insistent*) We're not there yet. After that interview you need to

announce some pretty impressive action. We have to make this stick,
we must show you're serious.

Jim Yes. An initiative?

Humphrey Yes.

Jim A working party?

Claire A bit lightweight.

Jim Task force.

Claire Not sure.

Jim Have we got enough in the kitty?

Bernard It could be one of those initiatives which you announce but
never actually spend the money ...

Claire Great! Like the one on child poverty.

Jim Maybe it should be a government committee?

Humphrey What about a Royal Commission?

Jim That's more like it. It won't report for three years. And if we put the
right people on it they won't agree about anything important. Right, a
Royal Commission.

Claire No, wait a minute, that makes it sound as if we think it's important
but not urgent.

Jim So what do you suggest?

Humphrey What about a global warming czar?

Jim Fine. Will that do it?

Humphrey I think it would need a bit more than that, Prime Minister.

Jim Such as?

Humphrey It will mean announcing quite a big unit. And an impressive
salary for the czar. To show how much importance you place upon the
appointment.

Jim No problem. Who should it be?

Humphrey It can't be a political figure. Too divisive. Someone impartial.
Someone who knows how to operate the levers of power. Engage the
gears of the Whitehall machine. Drive the engine of government.

Jim That's quite a tall order. Anyone got any ideas? (*He stares at
Humphrey*) Humphrey! Could you...?

Humphrey (*as if surprised*) Oh. Yes, Prime Minister.

Black-out

CURTAIN

FURNITURE AND PROPERTY LIST

If possible, monitors should be present in the auditorium to allow the audience to watch the live BBC interview in ACT II, Scene 2

ACT I

SCENE 1

On stage: Desk. *On it*: telephone, paper clips, red binder
Chair
Globe
Sitting area including sofa
Coffee table
Side table
TV
Remote control for TV
Five red boxes containing files
Evening Standard (for **Bernard**)
Scotch
Whisky glasses
Remote control for slides
Practical electrically operated screen for slides

Off stage: Briefcase (**Jim**)

Personal: **Humphrey**: handkerchief (in breast pocket)
Bernard: BlackBerry

SCENE 2

Strike: Red boxes
Jim's whisky glass

Personal: **Jim**: BlackBerry

ACT II

SCENE 1

Set: Fill five whisky glasses. Set three on coffee table,
              one on desk and one on side table

Off stage: Wet umbrella (**Claire**)
              Wellies (**Claire**)

Personal: **Bernard**: notepad and pen

SCENE 2

Set: Union Jack
              EU Flag
              Practical digital cameras broadcasting to auditorium monitors
              Champagne and glasses

Off stage: Red box (**Claire**)

LIGHTING PLOT

Property fittings required: nil
Interior, the same throughout.

ACT I, SCENE 1

To open: Interior lighting, late afternoon

Cue 1	**Humphrey** exits	(Page 14)
	Black-out	

ACT I, SCENE 2

To open: Interior lighting, night

Cue 2	**Humphrey**: "Quite."	(Page 37)
	Black-out	

ACT II, SCENE 1

To open: Interior lighting, night

Cue 3	**Jim**: "See if He answers."	(Page 49)
	Huge flash of lightning	
Cue 4	**Bernard**: "No way he'll approve."	(Page 49)
	More tremendous lightning	
Cue 5	**Jim** waits at the window	(Page 50)
	Final flicker of distant lightning	
Cue 6	**Jim** nods hopelessly	(Page 61)
	Huge flash of lightning. Lights flicker and go out	
Cue 7	**Humphrey**: "... the answer to all your problems."	(Page 61)
	Lights flicker back on	
Cue 8	**Jim**: "That's all that matters."	(Page 63)
	Black-out	

ACT II, SCENE 2

To open: Interior lighting, morning

Cue 9   **Humphrey**: "Yes, Prime Minister."   (Page 66)
               Black-out

EFFECTS PLOT

ACT I

Cue 1	To open ACT I, Scene 1 **TV Newsreader** *recording as script p.1*	(Page 1)
Cue 2	**Humphrey** switches off the TV with the remote *Cut TV recording*	(Page 1)
Cue 3	**Bernard** presses the speakerphone button **Robin**'s *voice recording as script p.17*	(Page 16)
Cue 4	**Bernard**: "It's business as usual." **Robin**'s *first voice recording as script p.17*	(Page 17)
Cue 5	**Bernard**: "Next?" **Robin**'s *second voice recording as script p.17*	(Page 17)
Cue 6	**Bernard**: "... within the Community." **Robin**'s *third voice recording as script p.17*	(Page 17)
Cue 7	**Bernard**: "... when the time is ripe." **Robin**'s *fourth voice recording as script p.18*	(Page 17)
Cue 8	**Jim** and **Claire**: "FIVE!" **Robin**'s *fifth voice recording as script p.18*	(Page 18)
Cue 9	**Jim**: "... Broadcasting House and the TV Centre." *Phone rings*	(Page 18)
Cue 10	**Claire**: "Hope it rains." *Phone rings*	(Page 29)

ACT II

Cue 11	**Jim**: "See if He answers." *Loud crack of thunder, followed by sudden rain against the windows*	(Page 49)
Cue 12	**Bernard**: "No way he'll approve." *More tremendous thunder*	(Page 49)